30 Days with Jesus

THOMAS NELSON PUBLISHERS
Nashville

30 Days with Jesus

Printed in the United States of America
2 3 4 5 6 7 8 9 10 – 05 04 03 02 01 00

Contents

V

Introduction

Hey! You've got to read this!

This book is all about a challenge: To get *extreme for Jesus* by spending 30 days with Him in the Word of God!

Have you ever wondered what it would have been like to be a disciple and to really live with Jesus? To look right into His face every day and hear the things He was saying? To follow Him wherever He went, to do without the things He did without, to suffer the same disrespect and humiliation He did? To belong to Him totally, no matter what the cost?

It's one thing to be a believer—and a great thing too! There's nothing like having faith in Jesus, receiving forgiveness and eternal life because of what He did when He died on a cross for us.

But are you a *follower* of Jesus? Is your life radically and totally turned over to Him? That's what being *extreme for Jesus* is all about. Just being real, not phony. One face, not two. No half-way measures, just honest to God, all the way, stop at nothing, do what He says, sold out for Him!

It's about letting Jesus change the kind of person you are. It means giving everything to Him. Your relationships, your feelings, your school, your future, everything. Sometimes it means confronting. Sometimes it means doing the right thing and not following the crowd. Sometimes it just means caring about somebody who needs a little love. Are you ready for it?

This book has 30 daily readings taken from the four Gospels of the New King James Version of the Bible. They take you through the life of Jesus. (We got them from the reading plan in *The Extreme Teen Bible*.) Each reading is followed by a devotion written especially for this book by a member of Audio Adrenaline, sharing about how that reading has influenced him and challenged him in his faith. You really feel like you're right there with the band, studying God's Word and talking about what it means in the real world!

Then there's space for you to write down what you believe God is telling you about how to get extreme for Jesus in your own life.

Can you handle it? Can you deal with spending 30 days learning how to be the kind of follower Jesus wants?

Then come on!

THE ETERNAL WORD

[1]In the beginning was the Word, and the Word was with God, and the Word was God. [2]He was in the beginning with God. [3]All things were made through Him, and without Him nothing was made that was made. [4]In Him was life, and the life was the light of men. [5]And the light shines in the darkness, and the darkness did not comprehend it.

JOHN'S WITNESS: THE TRUE LIGHT

[6]There was a man sent from God, whose name *was* John. [7]This man came for a witness, to bear witness of the Light, that all through him might believe. [8]He was not that Light, but *was sent* to bear witness of that Light. [9]That was the true Light which gives light to every man coming into the world.

[10]He was in the world, and the world was made through Him, and the world did not know Him. [11]He came to His own, and His own did not receive Him. [12]But as many as received Him, to them He gave the right to become children of God, to those who believe in His name: [13]who were born, not of blood, nor of the will of the flesh, nor of the will of man, but of God.

THE WORD BECOMES FLESH

[14]And the Word became flesh and dwelt among us, and we beheld His glory, the glory as of the only begotten of the Father, full of grace and truth.

[15]John bore witness of Him and cried out, saying, "This was He of whom I said, 'He who comes after me is preferred before me, for He was before me.' "

[16]And of His fullness we have all received, and grace for grace. [17]For the law was given through Moses, *but* grace and truth came through Jesus Christ. [18]No one has seen God at any time. The only begotten Son, who is in the bosom of the Father, He has declared *Him*.

A VOICE IN THE WILDERNESS

[19]Now this is the testimony of John, when the Jews sent priests and Levites from Jerusalem to ask him, "Who are you?"

[20]He confessed, and did not deny, but confessed, "I am not the Christ."

[21]And they asked him, "What then? Are you Elijah?"

He said, "I am not."

"Are you the Prophet?"

And he answered, "No."

[22]Then they said to him, "Who are you, that we may give an answer to those who sent us? What do you say about yourself?"

[23]He said: "I *am*

'The voice of one crying in the
    wilderness:
"Make straight the way of the
    LORD," '

as the prophet Isaiah said."

[24]Now those who were sent were from the Pharisees. [25]And they asked him, saying, "Why then do you baptize if you are not the Christ, nor Elijah, nor the Prophet?"

[26]John answered them, saying, "I baptize with water, but there stands One among you whom you do not know. [27]It is He who, coming after me,

is preferred before me, whose sandal strap I am not worthy to loose."

²⁸These things were done in Bethabara beyond the Jordan, where John was baptizing.

THE LAMB OF GOD

²⁹The next day John saw Jesus coming toward him, and said, "Behold! The Lamb of God who takes away the sin of the world! ³⁰This is He of whom I said, 'After me comes a Man who is preferred before me, for He was before me.' ³¹I did not know Him; but that He should be revealed to Israel, therefore I came baptizing with water."

³²And John bore witness, saying, "I saw the Spirit descending from heaven like a dove, and He remained upon Him. ³³I did not know Him, but He who sent me to baptize with water said to me, 'Upon whom you see the Spirit descending, and remaining on Him, this is He who baptizes with the Holy Spirit.' ³⁴And I have seen and testified that this is the Son of God."

THE FIRST DISCIPLES

³⁵Again, the next day, John stood with two of his disciples. ³⁶And looking at Jesus as He walked, he said, "Behold the Lamb of God!"

³⁷The two disciples heard him speak, and they followed Jesus. ³⁸Then Jesus turned, and seeing them following, said to them, "What do you seek?"

They said to Him, "Rabbi" (which is to say, when translated, Teacher), "where are You staying?"

³⁹He said to them, "Come and see." They came and saw where He was staying, and remained with Him that day (now it was about the tenth hour).

⁴⁰One of the two who heard John

speak, and followed Him, was Andrew, Simon Peter's brother. ⁴¹He first found his own brother Simon, and said to him, "We have found the Messiah" (which is translated, the Christ). ⁴²And he brought him to Jesus.

Now when Jesus looked at him, He said, "You are Simon the son of Jonah. You shall be called Cephas" (which is translated, A Stone).

PHILIP AND NATHANAEL

⁴³The following day Jesus wanted to go to Galilee, and He found Philip and said to him, "Follow Me." ⁴⁴Now Philip was from Bethsaida, the city of Andrew and Peter. ⁴⁵Philip found Nathanael and said to him, "We have found Him of whom Moses in the law, and also the prophets, wrote— Jesus of Nazareth, the son of Joseph."

⁴⁶And Nathanael said to him, "Can anything good come out of Nazareth?"

Philip said to him, "Come and see."

⁴⁷Jesus saw Nathanael coming toward Him, and said of him, "Behold, an Israelite indeed, in whom is no deceit!"

⁴⁸Nathanael said to Him, "How do You know me?"

Jesus answered and said to him, "Before Philip called you, when you were under the fig tree, I saw you."

⁴⁹Nathanael answered and said to Him, "Rabbi, You are the Son of God! You are the King of Israel!"

⁵⁰Jesus answered and said to him, "Because I said to you, 'I saw you under the fig tree,' do you believe? You will see greater things than these." ⁵¹And He said to him, "Most assuredly, I say to you, hereafter you shall see heaven open, and the angels of God ascending and descending upon the Son of Man."

preparing the way

There are people whose job is to promote our concerts, preparing the way for our arrival into a city. They let others know about the show so that, hopefully, people will buy tickets and come see us play. Nobody will show up if they don't know we're coming. In a slightly uncomfortable comparison, that's like what John the Baptist did for Jesus. While we know that we're never gonna be as big as Jesus, it'd be cool to be a bit more like John the Baptist. Am I preparing the way for people to meet Christ? Can I do a better job pumping people up about the fact that Christ is here among us? Hearing how John was pretty radical makes me want to kick my efforts up a few notches. I want to be the radical locust-eating guy who reminds even believers to wake up, and see that God is right here walking among us. What can I say that would make people listen? How can I be so passionate about what God has done for me that other people would be interested in finding Him for themselves?

Tyler Burkum

How I'm getting more extreme for Jesus today:

_____

_____

_____

_____

_____

_____

_____

"Behold! The Lamb of God who takes away the sin of the world!"
(John 1:29b)

4

CHRIST BORN OF MARY

¹And it came to pass in those days *that* a decree went out from Caesar Augustus that all the world should be registered. ²This census first took place while Quirinius was governing Syria. ³So all went to be registered, everyone to his own city.

⁴Joseph also went up from Galilee, out of the city of Nazareth, into Judea, to the city of David, which is called Bethlehem, because he was of the house and lineage of David, ⁵to be registered with Mary, his betrothed wife, who was with child. ⁶So it was, that while they were there, the days were completed for her to be delivered. ⁷And she brought forth her firstborn Son, and wrapped Him in swaddling cloths, and laid Him in a manger, because there was no room for them in the inn.

GLORY IN THE HIGHEST

⁸Now there were in the same country shepherds living out in the fields, keeping watch over their flock by night. ⁹And behold, an angel of the Lord stood before them, and the glory of the Lord shone around them, and they were greatly afraid. ¹⁰Then the angel said to them, "Do not be afraid, for behold, I bring you good tidings of great joy which will be to all people. ¹¹For there is born to you this day in the city of David a Savior, who is Christ the Lord. ¹²And this *will be* the sign to you: You will find a Babe wrapped in swaddling cloths, lying in a manger."

¹³And suddenly there was with the angel a multitude of the heavenly host praising God and saying:

¹⁴"Glory to God in the highest,
And on earth peace, goodwill
    toward men!"

¹⁵So it was, when the angels had gone away from them into heaven, that the shepherds said to one another, "Let us now go to Bethlehem and see this thing that has come to pass, which the Lord has made known to us." ¹⁶And they came with haste and found Mary and Joseph, and the Babe lying in a manger. ¹⁷Now when they had seen *Him*, they made widely known the saying which was told them concerning this Child. ¹⁸And all those who heard *it* marveled at those things which were told them by the shepherds. ¹⁹But Mary kept all these things and pondered *them* in her heart. ²⁰Then the shepherds returned, glorifying and praising God for all the things that they had heard and seen, as it was told them.

CIRCUMCISION OF JESUS

²¹And when eight days were completed for the circumcision of the Child, His name was called JESUS, the name given by the angel before He was conceived in the womb.

JESUS PRESENTED IN THE TEMPLE

²²Now when the days of her purification according to the law of Moses were completed, they brought Him to Jerusalem to present *Him* to the Lord ²³(as it is written in the law of the Lord, "Every male who opens the womb shall be called holy to the LORD"), ²⁴and to offer a sacrifice according to what is said in the law of the Lord, "A pair of turtledoves or two young pigeons."

SIMEON SEES GOD'S SALVATION

²⁵And behold, there was a man in Jerusalem whose name was Simeon, and this man was just and devout, waiting for the Consolation of Israel, and the Holy Spirit was upon him. ²⁶And it had been revealed to him by the Holy Spirit that he would not see death before he had seen the Lord's Christ. ²⁷So he came by the Spirit into the temple. And when the parents brought in the Child Jesus, to do for Him according to the custom of the law, ²⁸he took Him up in his arms and blessed God and said:

²⁹"Lord, now You are letting Your
    servant depart in peace,
    According to Your word;
³⁰ For my eyes have seen Your
    salvation
³¹ Which You have prepared before
    the face of all peoples,
³² A light to *bring* revelation to the
    Gentiles,
    And the glory of Your people
    Israel."

³³And Joseph and His mother marveled at those things which were spoken of Him. ³⁴Then Simeon blessed them, and said to Mary His mother, "Behold, this *Child* is destined for the fall and rising of many in Israel, and for a sign which will be spoken against ³⁵(yes, a sword will pierce through your own soul also), that the thoughts of many hearts may be revealed."

ANNA BEARS WITNESS TO THE REDEEMER

³⁶Now there was one, Anna, a prophetess, the daughter of Phanuel, of the tribe of Asher. She was of a great age, and had lived with a husband seven years from her virginity; ³⁷and this woman *was* a widow of about eighty-four years, who did not depart from the temple, but served *God* with fastings and prayers night and day. ³⁸And coming in that instant she gave thanks to the Lord, and spoke of Him to all those who looked for redemption in Jerusalem.

THE FAMILY RETURNS TO NAZARETH

³⁹So when they had performed all things according to the law of the Lord, they returned to Galilee, to their *own* city, Nazareth. ⁴⁰And the Child grew and became strong in spirit, filled with wisdom; and the grace of God was upon Him.

THE BOY JESUS AMAZES THE SCHOLARS

⁴¹His parents went to Jerusalem every year at the Feast of the Passover. ⁴²And when He was twelve years old, they went up to Jerusalem according to the custom of the feast. ⁴³When they had finished the days, as they returned, the Boy Jesus lingered behind in Jerusalem. And Joseph and His mother did not know *it*; ⁴⁴but supposing Him to have been in the company, they went a day's journey, and sought Him among *their* relatives and acquaintances. ⁴⁵So when they did not find Him, they returned to Jerusalem, seeking Him. ⁴⁶Now so it was *that* after three days they found Him in the temple, sitting in the midst of the teachers, both listening to them and asking them questions. ⁴⁷And all who heard Him were astonished at His understanding and answers. ⁴⁸So when they saw Him, they were amazed; and His mother said to Him, "Son, why have You done this to us?

Look, Your father and I have sought You anxiously."

⁴⁹And He said to them, "Why did you seek Me? Did you not know that I must be about My Father's business?" ⁵⁰But they did not understand the statement which He spoke to them.

JESUS ADVANCES IN WISDOM AND FAVOR

⁵¹Then He went down with them and came to Nazareth, and was subject to them, but His mother kept all these things in her heart. ⁵²And Jesus increased in wisdom and stature, and in favor with God and men.

good tidings of great joy

I've heard this so many times, but it still blows me away how in Luke 2:8-9 the angel decided to appear to the shepherds out in the field. Why would God think that these guys were important enough to receive this divine revelation? God obviously had a plan for how He was going to glorify Himself through the appearance of the angel to the shepherds. But these were just normal guys like you and me. They weren't necessarily important to anybody in society. But still God chose them! This is such a reminder that God can use the little guy, or even the underdog. It's easy to think that you have to be really incredible at something for God to use you, when in fact He desires to use you right where you are. When God wants to tell you something He will come to you wherever you are. Do you think you have to be in a position of importance to other people before God will be interested in using you? What do you need to do to be ready to hear from God today?

Tyler Burkum

What God is telling me in His Word today:

_____

_____

_____

8

JOHN THE BAPTIST PREPARES THE WAY

¹The beginning of the gospel of Jesus Christ, the Son of God. ²As it is written in the Prophets:

"Behold, I send My messenger
  before Your face,
Who will prepare Your way before
  You."
³ "The voice of one crying in the
  wilderness:
'Prepare the way of the LORD;
Make His paths straight.' "

⁴John came baptizing in the wilderness and preaching a baptism of repentance for the remission of sins. ⁵Then all the land of Judea, and those from Jerusalem, went out to him and were all baptized by him in the Jordan River, confessing their sins.

⁶Now John was clothed with camel's hair and with a leather belt around his waist, and he ate locusts and wild honey. ⁷And he preached, saying, "There comes One after me who is mightier than I, whose sandal strap I am not worthy to stoop down and loose. ⁸I indeed baptized you with water, but He will baptize you with the Holy Spirit."

JOHN BAPTIZES JESUS

⁹It came to pass in those days *that* Jesus came from Nazareth of Galilee, and was baptized by John in the Jordan. ¹⁰And immediately, coming up from the water, He saw the heavens parting and the Spirit descending upon Him like a dove. ¹¹Then a voice came from heaven, "You are My beloved Son, in whom I am well pleased."

strange but true

It's amazing that John the Baptist would spend so much time talking about Jesus, preparing the way for His arrival, and then he would be allowed to actually baptize Him! John even confessed his humble position to the crowds, admitting that Jesus would actually be so much greater than himself. I'm sure people thought that John was already pretty crazy for eating locusts, but when he talked of this One who was coming after him, the people were probably slightly baffled and intrigued. It's kind of like when you hear a new CD by your favorite group that you want to tell all

continued on next page

your friends about. You'd never say, "It's just about as good as their last CD." You'd say, "It's so much better than their last! You've got to go buy it!" They would see how passionate you are about the music and would most likely want to experience it themselves. How can you tell your friends about Christ in a way that would be intriguing to them? Is He just another wise man? Or is He more important than any person that ever walked the planet?

Will McGinniss

•••◦●◦••••

How I'm taking up the challenge today:

_____

_____

_____

_____

_____

_____

_____

_____

_____

_____

_____

_____

_____

_____

_____

_____

_____

_____

_____

_____

_____

_____

_____

_____

_____

_____

_____

_____

_____

_____

_____

_____

_____

_____

_____

_____

_____

> "There comes One after me who is mightier than I, whose sandal strap I am not worthy to stoop down and loose."
> (Mark 1:7b)

SATAN TEMPTS JESUS

¹Then Jesus, being filled with the Holy Spirit, returned from the Jordan and was led by the Spirit into the wilderness, ²being tempted for forty days by the devil. And in those days He ate nothing, and afterward, when they had ended, He was hungry.

³And the devil said to Him, "If You are the Son of God, command this stone to become bread."

⁴But Jesus answered him, saying, "It is written, 'Man shall not live by bread alone, but by every word of God.' "

⁵Then the devil, taking Him up on a high mountain, showed Him all the kingdoms of the world in a moment of time. ⁶And the devil said to Him, "All this authority I will give You, and their glory; for *this* has been delivered to me, and I give it to whomever I wish. ⁷Therefore, if You will worship before me, all will be Yours."

⁸And Jesus answered and said to him, "Get behind Me, Satan! For it is written, 'You shall worship the LORD your God, and Him only you shall serve.' "

⁹Then he brought Him to Jerusalem, set Him on the pinnacle of the temple, and said to Him, "If You are the Son of God, throw Yourself down from here. ¹⁰For it is written:

'He shall give His angels charge over you,
To keep you,'

¹¹and,

'In *their* hands they shall bear you up,

Lest you dash your foot against a stone.' "

¹²And Jesus answered and said to him, "It has been said, 'You shall not tempt the LORD your God.' "

¹³Now when the devil had ended every temptation, he departed from Him until an opportune time.

JESUS BEGINS HIS GALILEAN MINISTRY

¹⁴Then Jesus returned in the power of the Spirit to Galilee, and news of Him went out through all the surrounding region. ¹⁵And He taught in their synagogues, being glorified by all.

JESUS REJECTED AT NAZARETH

¹⁶So He came to Nazareth, where He had been brought up. And as His custom was, He went into the synagogue on the Sabbath day, and stood up to read. ¹⁷And He was handed the book of the prophet Isaiah. And when He had opened the book, He found the place where it was written:

¹⁸"The Spirit of the LORD *is* upon Me,
Because He has anointed Me
To preach the gospel to *the* poor;
He has sent Me to heal the brokenhearted,
To proclaim liberty to *the* captives
And recovery of sight to *the* blind,
To set at liberty those who are oppressed;
¹⁹ To proclaim the acceptable year of the LORD."

²⁰Then He closed the book, and gave *it* back to the attendant and sat down. And the eyes of all who were in the

synagogue were fixed on Him. [21]And He began to say to them, "Today this Scripture is fulfilled in your hearing." [22]So all bore witness to Him, and marveled at the gracious words which proceeded out of His mouth. And they said, "Is this not Joseph's son?"

[23]He said to them, "You will surely say this proverb to Me, 'Physician, heal yourself! Whatever we have heard done in Capernaum, do also here in Your country.' " [24]Then He said, "Assuredly, I say to you, no prophet is accepted in his own country. [25]But I tell you truly, many widows were in Israel in the days of Elijah, when the heaven was shut up three years and six months, and there was a great famine throughout all the land; [26]but to none of them was Elijah sent except to Zarephath, *in the region* of Sidon, to a woman *who was* a widow. [27]And many lepers were in Israel in the time of Elisha the prophet, and none of them was cleansed except Naaman the Syrian."

[28]So all those in the synagogue, when they heard these things, were filled with wrath, [29]and rose up and thrust Him out of the city; and they led Him to the brow of the hill on which their city was built, that they might throw Him down over the cliff. [30]Then passing through the midst of them, He went His way.

JESUS CASTS OUT AN UNCLEAN SPIRIT

[31]Then He went down to Capernaum, a city of Galilee, and was teaching them on the Sabbaths. [32]And they were astonished at His teaching, for His word was with authority. [33]Now in the synagogue there was a man who had a spirit of an unclean demon. And he cried out with a loud voice, [34]saying, "Let *us* alone! What have we to do with You, Jesus of Nazareth? Did You come to destroy us? I know who You are—the Holy One of God!"

[35]But Jesus rebuked him, saying, "Be quiet, and come out of him!" And when the demon had thrown him in *their* midst, it came out of him and did not hurt him. [36]Then they were all amazed and spoke among themselves, saying, "What a word this *is!* For with authority and power He commands the unclean spirits, and they come out." [37]And the report about Him went out into every place in the surrounding region.

PETER'S MOTHER-IN-LAW HEALED

[38]Now He arose from the synagogue and entered Simon's house. But Simon's wife's mother was sick with a high fever, and they made request of Him concerning her. [39]So He stood over her and rebuked the fever, and it left her. And immediately she arose and served them.

MANY HEALED AFTER SABBATH SUNSET

[40]When the sun was setting, all those who had any that were sick with various diseases brought them to Him; and He laid His hands on every one of them and healed them. [41]And demons also came out of many, crying out and saying, "You are the Christ, the Son of God!"

And He, rebuking *them*, did not allow them to speak, for they knew that He was the Christ.

JESUS PREACHES IN GALILEE

[42]Now when it was day, He departed and went into a deserted place. And the crowd sought Him and came to Him, and tried to keep Him from

leaving them; [43]but He said to them, "I must preach the kingdom of God to the other cities also, because for this purpose I have been sent." [44]And He was preaching in the synagogues of Galilee.

led by the Spirit

The first verse of this intriguing chapter about temptation says that Jesus was led by the Spirit. If the Son of God allowed Himself to be led by the Spirit, how much more do I need to constantly choose to be led by the Spirit in everything I do? We play a lot of concerts all over the country, to a new group of people every time. Even though we play the same songs night after night, for a lot of people in the crowd the songs are brand new. I have to rely upon the Spirit to lead me through each night so I can play the songs like it's the very first time. For Jesus, being led by the Spirit didn't mean that He would be steered clear of temptation. But He had a way out of those difficult times armed with God's Word and the power of the Spirit. I can't rely upon my own strength to get me through any kind of struggle, onstage or off. In what areas do you need to allow yourself to be led by the Spirit?

Will McGinniss

How God's Spirit is leading me today:

_____

_____

_____

_____

_____

"The Spirit of the Lord is upon Me, because he has anointed Me...."
(Luke 4:18)

THE NEW BIRTH

¹There was a man of the Pharisees named Nicodemus, a ruler of the Jews. ²This man came to Jesus by night and said to Him, "Rabbi, we know that You are a teacher come from God; for no one can do these signs that You do unless God is with him."

³Jesus answered and said to him, "Most assuredly, I say to you, unless one is born again, he cannot see the kingdom of God."

⁴Nicodemus said to Him, "How can a man be born when he is old? Can he enter a second time into his mother's womb and be born?"

⁵Jesus answered, "Most assuredly, I say to you, unless one is born of water and the Spirit, he cannot enter the kingdom of God. ⁶That which is born of the flesh is flesh, and that which is born of the Spirit is spirit. ⁷Do not marvel that I said to you, 'You must be born again.' ⁸The wind blows where it wishes, and you hear the sound of it, but cannot tell where it comes from and where it goes. So is everyone who is born of the Spirit."

⁹Nicodemus answered and said to Him, "How can these things be?"

¹⁰Jesus answered and said to him, "Are you the teacher of Israel, and do not know these things? ¹¹Most assuredly, I say to you, We speak what We know and testify what We have seen, and you do not receive Our witness. ¹²If I have told you earthly things and you do not believe, how will you believe if I tell you heavenly things? ¹³No one has ascended to heaven but He who came down from heaven, *that is*, the Son of Man who is in heaven. ¹⁴And as Moses lifted up the serpent in the wilderness, even so must the Son of Man be lifted up, ¹⁵that whoever believes in Him should not perish but have eternal life. ¹⁶For God so loved the world that He gave His only begotten Son, that whoever believes in Him should not perish but have everlasting life. ¹⁷For God did not send His Son into the world to condemn the world, but that the world through Him might be saved.

¹⁸"He who believes in Him is not condemned; but he who does not believe is condemned already, because he has not believed in the name of the only begotten Son of God. ¹⁹And this is the condemnation, that the light has come into the world, and men loved darkness rather than light, because their deeds were evil. ²⁰For everyone practicing evil hates the light and does not come to the light, lest his deeds should be exposed. ²¹But he who does the truth comes to the light, that his deeds may be clearly seen, that they have been done in God."

JOHN THE BAPTIST EXALTS CHRIST

²²After these things Jesus and His disciples came into the land of Judea, and there He remained with them and baptized. ²³Now John also was baptizing in Aenon near Salim, because there was much water there. And they came and were baptized. ²⁴For John had not yet been thrown into prison.

²⁵Then there arose a dispute between *some* of John's disciples and the

Jews about purification. ²⁶And they came to John and said to him, "Rabbi, He who was with you beyond the Jordan, to whom you have testified —behold, He is baptizing, and all are coming to Him!"

²⁷John answered and said, "A man can receive nothing unless it has been given to him from heaven. ²⁸You yourselves bear me witness, that I said, 'I am not the Christ,' but, 'I have been sent before Him.' ²⁹He who has the bride is the bridegroom; but the friend of the bridegroom, who stands and hears him, rejoices greatly be-cause of the bridegroom's voice. Therefore this joy of mine is fulfilled. ³⁰He must increase, but I *must* de-crease. ³¹He who comes from above is above all; he who is of the earth is earthly and speaks of the earth. He who comes from heaven is above all. ³²And what He has seen and heard, that He testifies; and no one receives His testimony. ³³He who has received His testimony has certified that God is true. ³⁴For He whom God has sent speaks the words of God, for God does not give the Spirit by measure. ³⁵The Father loves the Son, and has given all things into His hand. ³⁶He who believes in the Son has everlast-ing life; and he who does not believe the Son shall not see life, but the wrath of God abides on him."

sharing your faith

John 3:16 has always been my "life verse." I call it the "football verse" because of the guy who always sits in the end zone holding up the John 3:16 sign. In my opinion, it's the most important sentence in the whole Bible, but I wonder how the guy holding up that sign has actually affected people? My family never went to church when I was growing up, but I knew the verse because of that guy. It's amazing to think that some-thing that simple, and even a bit crazy, could affect somebody's under-standing of God. There are so many simple things that people can do that really make a difference. Even saying, "God bless you," on an answering machine message may be just what somebody needs to hear! Sometimes I'm envious of people who appear to be bold in their faith. I want to be in that place where I am so constantly aware of the transforming power of God's love and grace that I can't help but be outspoken about it. What is holding you back from being bolder about your faith?

Ben Cissell

How I'm being bold in my faith today:

_____
_____
_____
_____
_____
_____
_____
_____
_____
_____
_____
_____
_____
_____
_____
_____
_____
_____
_____
_____

For God so loved the world that He gave His only begotten Son, that whoever believes in Him should not perish but have everlasting life. (John 3:16)

FOUR FISHERMEN CALLED AS DISCIPLES

¹So it was, as the multitude pressed about Him to hear the word of God, that He stood by the Lake of Gennesaret, ²and saw two boats standing by the lake; but the fishermen had gone from them and were washing *their* nets. ³Then He got into one of the boats, which was Simon's, and asked him to put out a little from the land. And He sat down and taught the multitudes from the boat.

⁴When He had stopped speaking, He said to Simon, "Launch out into the deep and let down your nets for a catch."

⁵But Simon answered and said to Him, "Master, we have toiled all night and caught nothing; nevertheless at Your word I will let down the net." ⁶And when they had done this, they caught a great number of fish, and their net was breaking. ⁷So they signaled to *their* partners in the other boat to come and help them. And they came and filled both the boats, so that they began to sink. ⁸When Simon Peter saw *it*, he fell down at Jesus' knees, saying, "Depart from me, for I am a sinful man, O Lord!"

⁹For he and all who were with him were astonished at the catch of fish which they had taken; ¹⁰and so also *were* James and John, the sons of Zebedee, who were partners with Simon. And Jesus said to Simon, "Do not be afraid. From now on you will catch men." ¹¹So when they had brought their boats to land, they forsook all and followed Him.

JESUS CLEANSES A LEPER

¹²And it happened when He was in a certain city, that behold, a man who was full of leprosy saw Jesus; and he fell on *his* face and implored Him, saying, "Lord, if You are willing, You can make me clean."

¹³Then He put out *His* hand and touched him, saying, "I am willing; be cleansed." Immediately the leprosy left him. ¹⁴And He charged him to tell no one, "But go and show yourself to the priest, and make an offering for your cleansing, as a testimony to them, just as Moses commanded."

¹⁵However, the report went around concerning Him all the more; and great multitudes came together to hear, and to be healed by Him of their infirmities. ¹⁶So He Himself *often* withdrew into the wilderness and prayed.

JESUS FORGIVES AND HEALS A PARALYTIC

¹⁷Now it happened on a certain day, as He was teaching, that there were Pharisees and teachers of the law sitting by, who had come out of every town of Galilee, Judea, and Jerusalem. And the power of the Lord was *present* to heal them. ¹⁸Then behold, men brought on a bed a man who was paralyzed, whom they sought to bring in and lay before Him. ¹⁹And when they could not find how they might bring him in, because of the crowd, they went up on the housetop and let him down with *his* bed through the tiling into the midst before Jesus.

[20]When He saw their faith, He said to him, "Man, your sins are forgiven you."

[21]And the scribes and the Pharisees began to reason, saying, "Who is this who speaks blasphemies? Who can forgive sins but God alone?"

[22]But when Jesus perceived their thoughts, He answered and said to them, "Why are you reasoning in your hearts? [23]Which is easier, to say, 'Your sins are forgiven you,' or to say, 'Rise up and walk'? [24]But that you may know that the Son of Man has power on earth to forgive sins"—He said to the man who was paralyzed, "I say to you, arise, take up your bed, and go to your house."

[25]Immediately he rose up before them, took up what he had been lying on, and departed to his own house, glorifying God. [26]And they were all amazed, and they glorified God and were filled with fear, saying, "We have seen strange things today!"

MATTHEW THE TAX COLLECTOR

[27]After these things He went out and saw a tax collector named Levi, sitting at the tax office. And He said to him, "Follow Me." [28]So he left all, rose up, and followed Him.

[29]Then Levi gave Him a great feast in his own house. And there were a great number of tax collectors and others who sat down with them. [30]And their scribes and the Pharisees complained against His disciples, saying, "Why do You eat and drink with tax collectors and sinners?"

[31]Jesus answered and said to them, "Those who are well have no need of a physician, but those who are sick. [32]I have not come to call the righteous, but sinners, to repentance."

JESUS IS QUESTIONED ABOUT FASTING

[33]Then they said to Him, "Why do the disciples of John fast often and make prayers, and likewise those of the Pharisees, but Yours eat and drink?"

[34]And He said to them, "Can you make the friends of the bridegroom fast while the bridegroom is with them? [35]But the days will come when the bridegroom will be taken away from them; then they will fast in those days."

[36]Then He spoke a parable to them: "No one puts a piece from a new garment on an old one; otherwise the new makes a tear, and also the piece that was taken out of the new does not match the old. [37]And no one puts new wine into old wineskins; or else the new wine will burst the wineskins and be spilled, and the wineskins will be ruined. [38]But new wine must be put into new wineskins, and both are preserved. [39]And no one, having drunk old wine, immediately desires new; for he says, 'The old is better.' "

willing and able

It's pretty cool how Jesus responded to the leper's request to heal him: "Lord, if You are willing." Of course Jesus was willing AND able to do a miracle for this man. There's no question that Jesus can also meet all our physical and spiritual needs, yet we still worry about what clothes to wear or when we're going to get something to eat when we're hungry. We even worry about how to be a strong Christian in school. Jesus is willing to help you whenever and wherever you need it. He would love it if you could adopt that same attitude to the people around you. God longs to be an active part of our lives, constantly showing us that we are special to Him. How can you show that to someone else? It's pretty easy to see the needs of people around us—many that we are actually able to meet. But most of the time we're not willing. Jesus answered the leper, "I am willing." Could you say the same?

Will McGinniss

How I'm willing to be used by Jesus today:

_____

_____

_____

_____

_____

_____

_____

He put out His hand and touched him, saying, "I am willing; be cleansed." (Luke 5:13a)

A SAMARITAN WOMAN MEETS HER MESSIAH

[1]Therefore, when the Lord knew that the Pharisees had heard that Jesus made and baptized more disciples than John [2](though Jesus Himself did not baptize, but His disciples), [3]He left Judea and departed again to Galilee. [4]But He needed to go through Samaria.

[5]So He came to a city of Samaria which is called Sychar, near the plot of ground that Jacob gave to his son Joseph. [6]Now Jacob's well was there. Jesus therefore, being wearied from *His* journey, sat thus by the well. It was about the sixth hour.

[7]A woman of Samaria came to draw water. Jesus said to her, "Give Me a drink." [8]For His disciples had gone away into the city to buy food.

[9]Then the woman of Samaria said to Him, "How is it that You, being a Jew, ask a drink from me, a Samaritan woman?" For Jews have no dealings with Samaritans.

[10]Jesus answered and said to her, "If you knew the gift of God, and who it is who says to you, 'Give Me a drink,' you would have asked Him, and He would have given you living water."

[11]The woman said to Him, "Sir, You have nothing to draw with, and the well is deep. Where then do You get that living water? [12]Are You greater than our father Jacob, who gave us the well, and drank from it himself, as well as his sons and his livestock?"

[13]Jesus answered and said to her, "Whoever drinks of this water will thirst again, [14]but whoever drinks of the water that I shall give him will never thirst. But the water that I shall give him will become in him a fountain of water springing up into everlasting life."

[15]The woman said to Him, "Sir, give me this water, that I may not thirst, nor come here to draw."

[16]Jesus said to her, "Go, call your husband, and come here."

[17]The woman answered and said, "I have no husband."

Jesus said to her, "You have well said, 'I have no husband,' [18]for you have had five husbands, and the one whom you now have is not your husband; in that you spoke truly."

[19]The woman said to Him, "Sir, I perceive that You are a prophet. [20]Our fathers worshiped on this mountain, and you *Jews* say that in Jerusalem is the place where one ought to worship."

[21]Jesus said to her, "Woman, believe Me, the hour is coming when you will neither on this mountain, nor in Jerusalem, worship the Father. [22]You worship what you do not know; we know what we worship, for salvation is of the Jews. [23]But the hour is coming, and now is, when the true worshipers will worship the Father in spirit and truth; for the Father is seeking such to worship Him. [24]God *is* Spirit, and those who worship Him must worship in spirit and truth."

[25]The woman said to Him, "I know that Messiah is coming" (who is called Christ). "When He comes, He will tell us all things."

[26]Jesus said to her, "I who speak to you am *He*."

THE WHITENED HARVEST

[27]And at this *point* His disciples came, and they marveled that He

talked with a woman; yet no one said, "What do You seek?" or, "Why are You talking with her?"

28The woman then left her waterpot, went her way into the city, and said to the men, 29"Come, see a Man who told me all things that I ever did. Could this be the Christ?" 30Then they went out of the city and came to Him.

31In the meantime His disciples urged Him, saying, "Rabbi, eat."

32But He said to them, "I have food to eat of which you do not know."

33Therefore the disciples said to one another, "Has anyone brought Him *anything* to eat?"

34Jesus said to them, "My food is to do the will of Him who sent Me, and to finish His work. 35Do you not say, 'There are still four months and *then* comes the harvest'? Behold, I say to you, lift up your eyes and look at the fields, for they are already white for harvest! 36And he who reaps receives wages, and gathers fruit for eternal life, that both he who sows and he who reaps may rejoice together. 37For in this the saying is true: 'One sows and another reaps.' 38I sent you to reap that for which you have not labored; others have labored, and you have entered into their labors."

THE SAVIOR OF THE WORLD

39And many of the Samaritans of that city believed in Him because of the word of the woman who testified, "He told me all that I *ever* did." 40So when the Samaritans had come to Him, they urged Him to stay with them; and He stayed there two days. 41And many more believed because of His own word.

42Then they said to the woman, "Now we believe, not because of what you said, for we ourselves have heard *Him* and we know that this is indeed the Christ, the Savior of the world."

WELCOME AT GALILEE

43Now after the two days He departed from there and went to Galilee. 44For Jesus Himself testified that a prophet has no honor in his own country. 45So when He came to Galilee, the Galileans received Him, having seen all the things He did in Jerusalem at the feast; for they also had gone to the feast.

A NOBLEMAN'S SON HEALED

46So Jesus came again to Cana of Galilee where He had made the water wine. And there was a certain nobleman whose son was sick at Capernaum. 47When he heard that Jesus had come out of Judea into Galilee, he went to Him and implored Him to come down and heal his son, for he was at the point of death. 48Then Jesus said to him, "Unless you *people* see signs and wonders, you will by no means believe."

49The nobleman said to Him, "Sir, come down before my child dies!"

50Jesus said to him, "Go your way; your son lives." So the man believed the word that Jesus spoke to him, and he went his way. 51And as he was now going down, his servants met him and told *him*, saying, "Your son lives!"

52Then he inquired of them the hour when he got better. And they said to him, "Yesterday at the seventh hour the fever left him." 53So the father knew that *it was* at the same hour in which Jesus said to him, "Your son lives." And he himself believed, and his whole household.

54This again *is* the second sign Jesus did when He had come out of Judea into Galilee.

reaching out

I love how Jesus was so radical—hanging out with the kind of people the religious people wouldn't have anything to do with. The Samaritan woman at the well was so surprised that He would talk with her. It's amazing how we're so threatened by people who are different from us. Even our churches can appear to be clubs for particular groups of people, or even certain races. When I was in Bible College, we once had a service where a bum walked in off the street and sat down in a pew. People were staring at him, afraid that he might do something crazy. As he stood up and walked toward the front, he said things that were confrontational about our attitudes toward him. He then began removing pieces of his heavily draped clothing, and finally a wig—revealing himself to be our pastor. It was such a strong message about judging other people that I'll never forget it. I want to be more like Jesus and reach out to people who might appear different from me. Who could you surprise today by taking the time to talk with them?

Will McGinniss

What Jesus is telling me about reaching out to others:

_____

_____

_____

_____

_____

_____

> "Whoever drinks of this water will thirst again, but whoever drinks of the water that I shall give him will never thirst."
> (John 4:13b, 14a)

JESUS IS LORD OF THE SABBATH

¹Now it happened on the second Sabbath after the first that He went through the grainfields. And His disciples plucked the heads of grain and ate *them,* rubbing *them* in *their* hands. ²And some of the Pharisees said to them, "Why are you doing what is not lawful to do on the Sabbath?"

³But Jesus answering them said, "Have you not even read this, what David did when he was hungry, he and those who were with him: ⁴how he went into the house of God, took and ate the showbread, and also gave some to those with him, which is not lawful for any but the priests to eat?" ⁵And He said to them, "The Son of Man is also Lord of the Sabbath."

HEALING ON THE SABBATH

⁶Now it happened on another Sabbath, also, that He entered the synagogue and taught. And a man was there whose right hand was withered. ⁷So the scribes and Pharisees watched Him closely, whether He would heal on the Sabbath, that they might find an accusation against Him. ⁸But He knew their thoughts, and said to the man who had the withered hand, "Arise and stand here." And he arose and stood. ⁹Then Jesus said to them, "I will ask you one thing: Is it lawful on the Sabbath to do good or to do evil, to save life or to destroy?" ¹⁰And when He had looked around at them all, He said to the man, "Stretch out your hand." And he did so, and his hand was restored as whole as the other. ¹¹But they were filled with rage, and discussed with one another what they might do to Jesus.

THE TWELVE APOSTLES

¹²Now it came to pass in those days that He went out to the mountain to pray, and continued all night in prayer to God. ¹³And when it was day, He called His disciples to *Himself;* and from them He chose twelve whom He also named apostles: ¹⁴Simon, whom He also named Peter, and Andrew his brother; James and John; Philip and Bartholomew; ¹⁵Matthew and Thomas; James the *son* of Alphaeus, and Simon called the Zealot; ¹⁶Judas *the son* of James, and Judas Iscariot who also became a traitor.

JESUS HEALS A GREAT MULTITUDE

¹⁷And He came down with them and stood on a level place with a crowd of His disciples and a great multitude of people from all Judea and Jerusalem, and from the seacoast of Tyre and Sidon, who came to hear Him and be healed of their diseases, ¹⁸as well as those who were tormented with unclean spirits. And they were healed. ¹⁹And the whole multitude sought to touch Him, for power went out from Him and healed *them* all.

THE BEATITUDES

²⁰Then He lifted up His eyes toward His disciples, and said:

"Blessed *are you* poor,
   For yours is the kingdom of
      God.

²¹ Blessed *are you* who hunger now,
   For you shall be filled.
 Blessed *are you* who weep now,
   For you shall laugh.
²² Blessed are you when men hate
     you,
   And when they exclude you,
   And revile *you*, and cast out your
     name as evil,
   For the Son of Man's sake.
²³ Rejoice in that day and leap for
     joy!
   For indeed your reward *is* great
     in heaven,
   For in like manner their fathers
     did to the prophets.

JESUS PRONOUNCES WOES

²⁴"But woe to you who are rich,
   For you have received your
     consolation.
²⁵ Woe to you who are full,
   For you shall hunger.
 Woe to you who laugh now,
   For you shall mourn and weep.
²⁶ Woe to you when all men speak
     well of you,
   For so did their fathers to the
     false prophets.

LOVE YOUR ENEMIES

²⁷"But I say to you who hear: Love your enemies, do good to those who hate you, ²⁸bless those who curse you, and pray for those who spitefully use you. ²⁹To him who strikes you on the *one* cheek, offer the other also. And from him who takes away your cloak, do not withhold *your* tunic either. ³⁰Give to everyone who asks of you. And from him who takes away your goods do not ask *them* back. ³¹And just as you want men to do to you, you also do to them likewise.

³²"But if you love those who love you, what credit is that to you? For even sinners love those who love them. ³³And if you do good to those who do good to you, what credit is that to you? For even sinners do the same. ³⁴And if you lend *to those* from whom you hope to receive back, what credit is that to you? For even sinners lend to sinners to receive as much back. ³⁵But love your enemies, do good, and lend, hoping for nothing in return; and your reward will be great, and you will be sons of the Most High. For He is kind to the unthankful and evil. ³⁶Therefore be merciful, just as your Father also is merciful.

DO NOT JUDGE

³⁷"Judge not, and you shall not be judged. Condemn not, and you shall not be condemned. Forgive, and you will be forgiven. ³⁸Give, and it will be given to you: good measure, pressed down, shaken together, and running over will be put into your bosom. For with the same measure that you use, it will be measured back to you."

³⁹And He spoke a parable to them: "Can the blind lead the blind? Will they not both fall into the ditch? ⁴⁰A disciple is not above his teacher, but everyone who is perfectly trained will be like his teacher. ⁴¹And why do you look at the speck in your brother's eye, but do not perceive the plank in your own eye? ⁴²Or how can you say to your brother, 'Brother, let me remove the speck that *is* in your eye,' when you yourself do not see the plank that *is* in your own eye? Hypocrite! First remove the plank from your own eye, and then you will see clearly to remove the speck that is in your brother's eye.

A TREE IS KNOWN BY ITS FRUIT

⁴³"For a good tree does not bear bad fruit, nor does a bad tree bear good fruit. ⁴⁴For every tree is known by its own fruit. For *men* do not gather figs from thorns, nor do they gather grapes from a bramble bush. ⁴⁵A good man out of the good treasure of his heart brings forth good; and an evil man out of the evil treasure of his heart brings forth evil. For out of the abundance of the heart his mouth speaks.

BUILD ON THE ROCK

⁴⁶"But why do you call Me 'Lord, Lord,' and not do the things which I say? ⁴⁷Whoever comes to Me, and hears My sayings and does them, I will show you whom he is like: ⁴⁸He is like a man building a house, who dug deep and laid the foundation on the rock. And when the flood arose, the stream beat vehemently against that house, and could not shake it, for it was founded on the rock. ⁴⁹But he who heard and did nothing is like a man who built a house on the earth without a foundation, against which the stream beat vehemently; and im–mediately it fell. And the ruin of that house was great."

seeking God's wisdom

DAY 8

I need to continually look at Jesus as the example for how to live my life. Luke 6:12-13 explains how Jesus was faced with the task of choosing His disciples and apostles. You'd think that He could just rely upon God's power in Him to make the right decision. But not settling for that, He chose to go out to the mountain and pray to God all night. Jesus was praying all the time. He would continually slip away from the disciples and pray. His life was permeated with prayer. He would pray all the time to be in complete alignment with His Father's heart and will. This is what I need to be doing as well. I so often neglect to spend the proper amount of time in prayer. I choose to rely upon my own good judgment and understanding instead of admitting to God that I need to completely rely upon Him. Are our lives so busy these days that even Jesus, if He were on earth today, wouldn't be able to get away to the mountain to pray all night? Seek to be like Jesus today, and pursue a deepened intimacy with the Father through prayer.

Bob Herdman

What Jesus is showing me about prayer today:

He went out to the mountain
to pray, and continued all
night in prayer to God.
(Luke 6:12b)

JESUS HEALS A CENTURION'S SERVANT

[1]Now when He concluded all His sayings in the hearing of the people, He entered Capernaum. [2]And a certain centurion's servant, who was dear to him, was sick and ready to die. [3]So when he heard about Jesus, he sent elders of the Jews to Him, pleading with Him to come and heal his servant. [4]And when they came to Jesus, they begged Him earnestly, saying that the one for whom He should do this was deserving, [5]"for he loves our nation, and has built us a synagogue."

[6]Then Jesus went with them. And when He was already not far from the house, the centurion sent friends to Him, saying to Him, "Lord, do not trouble Yourself, for I am not worthy that You should enter under my roof. [7]Therefore I did not even think myself worthy to come to You. But say the word, and my servant will be healed. [8]For I also am a man placed under authority, having soldiers under me. And I say to one, 'Go,' and he goes; and to another, 'Come,' and he comes; and to my servant, 'Do this,' and he does *it*."

[9]When Jesus heard these things, He marveled at him, and turned around and said to the crowd that followed Him, "I say to you, I have not found such great faith, not even in Israel!" [10]And those who were sent, returning to the house, found the servant well who had been sick.

JESUS RAISES THE SON OF THE WIDOW OF NAIN

[11]Now it happened, the day after, *that* He went into a city called Nain; and many of His disciples went with Him, and a large crowd. [12]And when He came near the gate of the city, behold, a dead man was being carried out, the only son of his mother; and she was a widow. And a large crowd from the city was with her. [13]When the Lord saw her, He had compassion on her and said to her, "Do not weep." [14]Then He came and touched the open coffin, and those who carried *him* stood still. And He said, "Young man, I say to you, arise." [15]So he who was dead sat up and began to speak. And He presented him to his mother.

[16]Then fear came upon all, and they glorified God, saying, "A great prophet has risen up among us"; and, "God has visited His people." [17]And this report about Him went throughout all Judea and all the surrounding region.

JOHN THE BAPTIST SENDS MESSENGERS TO JESUS

[18]Then the disciples of John reported to him concerning all these things. [19]And John, calling two of his disciples to *him*, sent *them* to Jesus, saying, "Are You the Coming One, or do we look for another?"

[20]When the men had come to Him, they said, "John the Baptist has sent us to You, saying, 'Are You the Coming One, or do we look for another?' " [21]And that very hour He cured many of infirmities, afflictions, and evil spirits; and to many blind He gave sight. [22]Jesus answered and said to them, "Go and tell John the things you have seen and heard: that *the* blind see, *the* lame walk, *the* lepers are cleansed, *the* deaf hear, *the* dead are raised, *the* poor have the gospel preached to them.

²³And blessed is *he* who is not offended because of Me."

²⁴When the messengers of John had departed, He began to speak to the multitudes concerning John: "What did you go out into the wilderness to see? A reed shaken by the wind? ²⁵But what did you go out to see? A man clothed in soft garments? Indeed those who are gorgeously appareled and live in luxury are in kings' courts. ²⁶But what did you go out to see? A prophet? Yes, I say to you, and more than a prophet. ²⁷This is *he* of whom it is written:

'Behold, I send My messenger
    before Your face,
Who will prepare Your way before
    You.'

²⁸For I say to you, among those born of women there is not a greater prophet than John the Baptist; but he who is least in the kingdom of God is greater than he." ²⁹And when all the people heard *Him*, even the tax collectors justified God, having been baptized with the baptism of John. ³⁰But the Pharisees and lawyers rejected the will of God for themselves, not having been baptized by him.

³¹And the Lord said, "To what then shall I liken the men of this generation, and what are they like? ³²They are like children sitting in the marketplace and calling to one another, saying:

'We played the flute for you,
    And you did not dance;
We mourned to you,
    And you did not weep.'

³³For John the Baptist came neither eating bread nor drinking wine, and you say, 'He has a demon.' ³⁴The Son of Man has come eating and drinking, and you say, 'Look, a glutton and a winebibber, a friend of tax collectors and sinners!' ³⁵But wisdom is justified by all her children."

A SINFUL WOMAN FORGIVEN

³⁶Then one of the Pharisees asked Him to eat with him. And He went to the Pharisee's house, and sat down to eat. ³⁷And behold, a woman in the city who was a sinner, when she knew that *Jesus* sat at the table in the Pharisee's house, brought an alabaster flask of fragrant oil, ³⁸and stood at His feet behind *Him* weeping; and she began to wash His feet with her tears, and wiped *them* with the hair of her head; and she kissed His feet and anointed *them* with the fragrant oil. ³⁹Now when the Pharisee who had invited Him saw *this*, he spoke to himself, saying, "This Man, if He were a prophet, would know who and what manner of woman *this is* who is touching Him, for she is a sinner."

⁴⁰And Jesus answered and said to him, "Simon, I have something to say to you."

So he said, "Teacher, say it."

⁴¹"There was a certain creditor who had two debtors. One owed five hundred denarii, and the other fifty. ⁴²And when they had nothing with which to repay, he freely forgave them both. Tell Me, therefore, which of them will love him more?"

⁴³Simon answered and said, "I suppose the *one* whom he forgave more."

And He said to him, "You have rightly judged." ⁴⁴Then He turned to the woman and said to Simon, "Do you see this woman? I entered your house; you gave Me no water for My feet, but she has washed My feet with her tears and wiped *them* with the hair of her head. ⁴⁵You gave Me no kiss, but this woman has not ceased to kiss My feet since the time I came in. ⁴⁶You did not anoint My head with oil, but this woman has anointed My feet with fragrant oil. ⁴⁷Therefore I say to you, her sins, *which are* many, are forgiven, for she loved much. But to whom little is forgiven, *the same* loves little."

⁴⁸Then He said to her, "Your sins are forgiven."

⁴⁹And those who sat at the table with Him began to say to themselves, "Who is this who even forgives sins?"

⁵⁰Then He said to the woman, "Your faith has saved you. Go in peace."

show God's love

I'm probably not alone in this, but growing up, it seems that parents can make it very clear that there are certain people you should stay away from. Perhaps those people are the ones who might possibly be a negative influence on you because of their personal lifestyle choices. Of course, your parents are only trying to protect you. Believe it or not, those are the people that Jesus hung around with. The Bible is filled with stories of how He was judged for hanging out with the real blatant sinners. His example proves that we need to be seeking relationships with people who might never be exposed to the gospel. I have some neighbors who aren't Christians. My job is not to take the Bible over to them and quote Scripture, but rather to be their friend and build a relationship. We need to be a light to the world, being their friends and showing them love. It doesn't mean that we have to condone or agree with their choices, but we do have to always be ready to give a reason for the love that we have for them.

Bob Herdman

How I'm showing God's love to others:

_____

_____

_____

_____

_____

_____

_____

_____

_____

_____

_____

_____

_____

_____

_____

_____

_____

_____

_____

"Her sins, which are many, are forgiven, for she loved much. But to whom little is forgiven, the same loves little."
(Luke 7:47b)

MANY WOMEN MINISTER TO JESUS

¹Now it came to pass, afterward, that He went through every city and village, preaching and bringing the glad tidings of the kingdom of God. And the twelve *were* with Him, ²and certain women who had been healed of evil spirits and infirmities—Mary called Magdalene, out of whom had come seven demons, ³and Joanna the wife of Chuza, Herod's steward, and Susanna, and many others who provided for Him from their substance.

THE PARABLE OF THE SOWER

⁴And when a great multitude had gathered, and they had come to Him from every city, He spoke by a parable: ⁵"A sower went out to sow his seed. And as he sowed, some fell by the wayside; and it was trampled down, and the birds of the air devoured it. ⁶Some fell on rock; and as soon as it sprang up, it withered away because it lacked moisture. ⁷And some fell among thorns, and the thorns sprang up with it and choked it. ⁸But others fell on good ground, sprang up, and yielded a crop a hundredfold." When He had said these things He cried, "He who has ears to hear, let him hear!"

THE PURPOSE OF PARABLES

⁹Then His disciples asked Him, saying, "What does this parable mean?" ¹⁰And He said, "To you it has been given to know the mysteries of the kingdom of God, but to the rest *it is given* in parables, that

'Seeing they may not see,
 And hearing they may not
    understand.'

THE PARABLE OF THE SOWER EXPLAINED

¹¹"Now the parable is this: The seed is the word of God. ¹²Those by the wayside are the ones who hear; then the devil comes and takes away the word out of their hearts, lest they should believe and be saved. ¹³But the ones on the rock *are those* who, when they hear, receive the word with joy; and these have no root, who believe for a while and in time of temptation fall away. ¹⁴Now the ones *that* fell among thorns are those who, when they have heard, go out and are choked with cares, riches, and pleasures of life, and bring no fruit to maturity. ¹⁵But the ones *that* fell on the good ground are those who, having heard the word with a noble and good heart, keep *it* and bear fruit with patience.

THE PARABLE OF THE REVEALED LIGHT

¹⁶"No one, when he has lit a lamp, covers it with a vessel or puts *it* under a bed, but sets *it* on a lampstand, that those who enter may see the light. ¹⁷For nothing is secret that will not be revealed, nor *anything* hidden that will not be known and come to light. ¹⁸Therefore take heed how you hear. For whoever has, to him *more* will be given; and whoever does not have, even what he seems to have will be taken from him."

JESUS' MOTHER AND BROTHERS COME TO HIM

¹⁹Then His mother and brothers came to Him, and could not approach Him because of the crowd. ²⁰And it

was told Him *by some*, who said, "Your mother and Your brothers are standing outside, desiring to see You."

[21]But He answered and said to them, "My mother and My brothers are these who hear the word of God and do it."

WIND AND WAVE OBEY JESUS

[22]Now it happened, on a certain day, that He got into a boat with His disciples. And He said to them, "Let us cross over to the other side of the lake." And they launched out. [23]But as they sailed He fell asleep. And a windstorm came down on the lake, and they were filling *with water*, and were in jeopardy. [24]And they came to Him and awoke Him, saying, "Master, Master, we are perishing!"

Then He arose and rebuked the wind and the raging of the water. And they ceased, and there was a calm. [25]But He said to them, "Where is your faith?"

And they were afraid, and marveled, saying to one another, "Who can this be? For He commands even the winds and water, and they obey Him!"

A DEMON-POSSESSED MAN HEALED

[26]Then they sailed to the country of the Gadarenes, which is opposite Galilee. [27]And when He stepped out on the land, there met Him a certain man from the city who had demons for a long time. And he wore no clothes, nor did he live in a house but in the tombs. [28]When he saw Jesus, he cried out, fell down before Him, and with a loud voice said, "What have I to do with You, Jesus, Son of the Most High God? I beg You, do not torment me!" [29]For He had commanded the unclean spirit to come out of the man.

For it had often seized him, and he was kept under guard, bound with chains and shackles; and he broke the bonds and was driven by the demon into the wilderness.

[30]Jesus asked him, saying, "What is your name?"

And he said, "Legion," because many demons had entered him. [31]And they begged Him that He would not command them to go out into the abyss.

[32]Now a herd of many swine was feeding there on the mountain. So they begged Him that He would permit them to enter them. And He permitted them. [33]Then the demons went out of the man and entered the swine, and the herd ran violently down the steep place into the lake and drowned.

[34]When those who fed *them* saw what had happened, they fled and told *it* in the city and in the country. [35]Then they went out to see what had happened, and came to Jesus, and found the man from whom the demons had departed, sitting at the feet of Jesus, clothed and in his right mind. And they were afraid. [36]They also who had seen *it* told them by what means he who had been demon-possessed was healed. [37]Then the whole multitude of the surrounding region of the Gadarenes asked Him to depart from them, for they were seized with great fear. And He got into the boat and returned.

[38]Now the man from whom the demons had departed begged Him that he might be with Him. But Jesus sent him away, saying, [39]"Return to your own house, and tell what great things God has done for you." And he went his way and proclaimed throughout the whole city what great things Jesus had done for him.

A GIRL RESTORED TO LIFE AND A WOMAN HEALED

⁴⁰So it was, when Jesus returned, that the multitude welcomed Him, for they were all waiting for Him. ⁴¹And behold, there came a man named Jairus, and he was a ruler of the synagogue. And he fell down at Jesus' feet and begged Him to come to his house, ⁴²for he had an only daughter about twelve years of age, and she was dying.

But as He went, the multitudes thronged Him. ⁴³Now a woman, having a flow of blood for twelve years, who had spent all her livelihood on physicians and could not be healed by any, ⁴⁴came from behind and touched the border of His garment. And immediately her flow of blood stopped.

⁴⁵And Jesus said, "Who touched Me?"

When all denied it, Peter and those with him said, "Master, the multitudes throng and press You, and You say, 'Who touched Me?' "

⁴⁶But Jesus said, "Somebody touched Me, for I perceived power going out from Me." ⁴⁷Now when the woman saw that she was not hidden, she came trembling; and falling down before Him, she declared to Him in the presence of all the people the reason she had touched Him and how she was healed immediately.

⁴⁸And He said to her, "Daughter, be of good cheer; your faith has made you well. Go in peace."

⁴⁹While He was still speaking, someone came from the ruler of the synagogue's *house*, saying to him, "Your daughter is dead. Do not trouble the Teacher."

⁵⁰But when Jesus heard *it*, He answered him, saying, "Do not be afraid; only believe, and she will be made well." ⁵¹When He came into the house, He permitted no one to go in except Peter, James, and John, and the father and mother of the girl. ⁵²Now all wept and mourned for her; but He said, "Do not weep; she is not dead, but sleeping." ⁵³And they ridiculed Him, knowing that she was dead.

⁵⁴But He put them all outside, took her by the hand and called, saying, "Little girl, arise." ⁵⁵Then her spirit returned, and she arose immediately. And He commanded that she be given *something* to eat. ⁵⁶And her parents were astonished, but He charged them to tell no one what had happened.

good soil

DAY 10

The parable of the sower points out to me how so often I don't allow myself to have good soil. I'm still growing in the understanding of my personal responsibility to tend to my own soil, making sure that the ground is able to grow the seeds that God wants to plant. It's nothing that

continued on next page

anybody else can do for me. Sometimes I hear a great message from the pastor, and the seeds just bounce right off me because I've been lying in a patch of weeds. I walk around with a hardened heart, not allowing myself to be very fertile ground. It's literally an everyday work to till the soil in my heart in order to stay open to the Word of God. I need to continually admit my need for Him. I can choose to put good things into my life by being responsible about what I watch, or what I say, or what I listen to. I need to be wise about what I put into my spirit, making sure that I'm not trying to live off of "empty calories" that may fill me up but leave me hungry. God is the ultimate nourishment for my hungry soul.

Tyler Burkum

How I'm learning more about Jesus today:

"The ones that fell on the good ground are those who, having heard the word with a noble and good heart, keep it and bear fruit with patience."
(Luke 8:14)

39

FEEDING THE FOUR THOUSAND

¹In those days, the multitude being very great and having nothing to eat, Jesus called His disciples *to Him* and said to them, ²"I have compassion on the multitude, because they have now continued with Me three days and have nothing to eat. ³And if I send them away hungry to their own houses, they will faint on the way; for some of them have come from afar."

⁴Then His disciples answered Him, "How can one satisfy these people with bread here in the wilderness?"

⁵He asked them, "How many loaves do you have?"

And they said, "Seven."

⁶So He commanded the multitude to sit down on the ground. And He took the seven loaves and gave thanks, broke *them* and gave *them* to His disciples to set before *them*; and they set *them* before the multitude. ⁷They also had a few small fish; and having blessed them, He said to set them also before *them*. ⁸So they ate and were filled, and they took up seven large baskets of leftover fragments. ⁹Now those who had eaten were about four thousand. And He sent them away, ¹⁰immediately got into the boat with His disciples, and came to the region of Dalmanutha.

THE PHARISEES SEEK A SIGN

¹¹Then the Pharisees came out and began to dispute with Him, seeking from Him a sign from heaven, testing Him. ¹²But He sighed deeply in His spirit, and said, "Why does this gener-ation seek a sign? Assuredly, I say to you, no sign shall be given to this generation."

BEWARE OF THE LEAVEN OF THE PHARISEES AND HEROD

¹³And He left them, and getting into the boat again, departed to the other side. ¹⁴Now the disciples had forgotten to take bread, and they did not have more than one loaf with them in the boat. ¹⁵Then He charged them, saying, "Take heed, beware of the leaven of the Pharisees and the leaven of Herod."

¹⁶And they reasoned among them-selves, saying, *"It is* because we have no bread."

¹⁷But Jesus, being aware of *it*, said to them, "Why do you reason because you have no bread? Do you not yet perceive nor understand? Is your heart still hardened? ¹⁸Having eyes, do you not see? And having ears, do you not hear? And do you not remember? ¹⁹When I broke the five loaves for the five thousand, how many baskets full of fragments did you take up?"

They said to Him, "Twelve."

²⁰"Also, when I broke the seven for the four thousand, how many large baskets full of fragments did you take up?"

And they said, "Seven."

²¹So He said to them, "How *is it* you do not understand?"

A BLIND MAN HEALED AT BETHSAIDA

²²Then He came to Bethsaida; and they brought a blind man to Him, and begged Him to touch him. ²³So He took the blind man by the hand and led him out of the town. And when He had spit on his eyes and put

His hands on him, He asked him if he saw anything.

²⁴And he looked up and said, "I see men like trees, walking."

²⁵Then He put *His* hands on his eyes again and made him look up. And he was restored and saw everyone clearly. ²⁶Then He sent him away to his house, saying, "Neither go into the town, nor tell anyone in the town."

PETER CONFESSES JESUS AS THE CHRIST

²⁷Now Jesus and His disciples went out to the towns of Caesarea Philippi; and on the road He asked His disciples, saying to them, "Who do men say that I am?"

²⁸So they answered, "John the Baptist; but some *say,* Elijah; and others, one of the prophets."

²⁹He said to them, "But who do you say that I am?"

Peter answered and said to Him, "You are the Christ."

³⁰Then He strictly warned them that they should tell no one about Him.

JESUS PREDICTS HIS DEATH AND RESURRECTION

³¹And He began to teach them that the Son of Man must suffer many things, and be rejected by the elders and chief priests and scribes, and be killed, and after three days rise again. ³²He spoke this word openly. Then Peter took Him aside and began to rebuke Him. ³³But when He had turned around and looked at His disciples, He rebuked Peter, saying, "Get behind Me, Satan! For you are not mindful of the things of God, but the things of men."

TAKE UP THE CROSS AND FOLLOW HIM

³⁴When He had called the people to *Himself,* with His disciples also, He said to them, "Whoever desires to come after Me, let him deny himself, and take up his cross, and follow Me. ³⁵For whoever desires to save his life will lose it, but whoever loses his life for My sake and the gospel's will save it. ³⁶For what will it profit a man if he gains the whole world, and loses his own soul? ³⁷Or what will a man give in exchange for his soul? ³⁸For whoever is ashamed of Me and My words in this adulterous and sinful generation, of him the Son of Man also will be ashamed when He comes in the glory of His Father with the holy angels."

seeing miracles

DAY 11

Jesus did some amazing things. I can't help but wonder if the disciples ever got calloused or lazy about the miracles that He did? If I was a disciple and had been walking through the sand and the heat, looking forward to calling it a day, and Jesus suddenly decided to stop and heal

continued on next page

another person, I think I'd be pretty irritated. I know I get that way now at times. I see God using us, even doing miracles, but I get tired and just want to get on the bus, or get home. It's so easy for me to take for granted what God has done and what He is doing for us even today. When I get focused on myself and how tired, lonely, or depressed I might be, I can only think of quitting. Then God usually uses someone to bring focus back to my life. Even though God doesn't have to do that, He still does. He never gets tired of seeing miracles. Even when I'm tired and ready to give up, He never gives up on me. In what ways do you take for granted the amazing wonder-working power of God?

Ben Cissell

What I'm experiencing with Jesus today:

_____

_____

_____

_____

_____

_____

_____

_____

_____

_____

_____

_____

_____

He put His hands on his eyes
again and made him look up.
And he was restored and saw
everyone clearly.
(Mark 8:25)

THE SEVENTY SENT OUT

¹After these things the Lord appointed seventy others also, and sent them two by two before His face into every city and place where He Himself was about to go. ²Then He said to them, "The harvest truly *is* great, but the laborers *are* few; therefore pray the Lord of the harvest to send out laborers into His harvest. ³Go your way; behold, I send you out as lambs among wolves. ⁴Carry neither money bag, knapsack, nor sandals; and greet no one along the road. ⁵But whatever house you enter, first say, 'Peace to this house.' ⁶And if a son of peace is there, your peace will rest on it; if not, it will return to you. ⁷And remain in the same house, eating and drinking such things as they give, for the laborer is worthy of his wages. Do not go from house to house. ⁸Whatever city you enter, and they receive you, eat such things as are set before you. ⁹And heal the sick there, and say to them, 'The kingdom of God has come near to you.' ¹⁰But whatever city you enter, and they do not receive you, go out into its streets and say, ¹¹'The very dust of your city which clings to us we wipe off against you. Nevertheless know this, that the kingdom of God has come near you.' ¹²But I say to you that it will be more tolerable in that Day for Sodom than for that city.

WOE TO THE IMPENITENT CITIES

¹³"Woe to you, Chorazin! Woe to you, Bethsaida! For if the mighty works which were done in you had been done in Tyre and Sidon, they would have repented long ago, sitting in sackcloth and ashes. ¹⁴But it will be more tolerable for Tyre and Sidon at the judgment than for you. ¹⁵And you, Capernaum, who are exalted to heaven, will be brought down to Hades. ¹⁶He who hears you hears Me, he who rejects you rejects Me, and he who rejects Me rejects Him who sent Me."

THE SEVENTY RETURN WITH JOY

¹⁷Then the seventy returned with joy, saying, "Lord, even the demons are subject to us in Your name."

¹⁸And He said to them, "I saw Satan fall like lightning from heaven. ¹⁹Behold, I give you the authority to trample on serpents and scorpions, and over all the power of the enemy, and nothing shall by any means hurt you. ²⁰Nevertheless do not rejoice in this, that the spirits are subject to you, but rather rejoice because your names are written in heaven."

JESUS REJOICES IN THE SPIRIT

²¹In that hour Jesus rejoiced in the Spirit and said, "I thank You, Father, Lord of heaven and earth, that You have hidden these things from *the* wise and prudent and revealed them to babes. Even so, Father, for so it seemed good in Your sight. ²²All things have been delivered to Me by My Father, and no one knows who the Son is except the Father, and who the Father is except the Son, and *the one* to whom the Son wills to reveal Him."

²³Then He turned to *His* disciples and said privately, "Blessed *are* the eyes which see the things you see; ²⁴for I tell you that many prophets and kings have desired to see what you see, and have not seen *it*, and to

hear what you hear, and have not heard *it*."

THE PARABLE OF THE GOOD SAMARITAN

²⁵And behold, a certain lawyer stood up and tested Him, saying, "Teacher, what shall I do to inherit eternal life?"

²⁶He said to him, "What is written in the law? What is your reading *of it?*"

²⁷So he answered and said, " 'You shall love the LORD your God with all your heart, with all your soul, with all your strength, and with all your mind,' and 'your neighbor as yourself.' "

²⁸And He said to him, "You have answered rightly; do this and you will live."

²⁹But he, wanting to justify himself, said to Jesus, "And who is my neighbor?"

³⁰Then Jesus answered and said: "A certain *man* went down from Jerusalem to Jericho, and fell among thieves, who stripped him of his clothing, wounded *him*, and departed, leaving *him* half dead. ³¹Now by chance a certain priest came down that road. And when he saw him, he passed by on the other side. ³²Likewise a Levite, when he arrived at the place, came and looked, and passed by on the other side. ³³But a certain Samaritan, as he journeyed, came where he was. And when he saw him, he had com-

passion. ³⁴So he went to *him* and bandaged his wounds, pouring on oil and wine; and he set him on his own animal, brought him to an inn, and took care of him. ³⁵On the next day, when he departed, he took out two denarii, gave *them* to the innkeeper, and said to him, 'Take care of him; and whatever more you spend, when I come again, I will repay you.' ³⁶So which of these three do you think was neighbor to him who fell among the thieves?"

³⁷And he said, "He who showed mercy on him."

Then Jesus said to him, "Go and do likewise."

MARY AND MARTHA WORSHIP AND SERVE

³⁸Now it happened as they went that He entered a certain village; and a certain woman named Martha welcomed Him into her house. ³⁹And she had a sister called Mary, who also sat at Jesus' feet and heard His word. ⁴⁰But Martha was distracted with much serving, and she approached Him and said, "Lord, do You not care that my sister has left me to serve alone? Therefore tell her to help me."

⁴¹And Jesus answered and said to her, "Martha, Martha, you are worried and troubled about many things. ⁴²But one thing is needed, and Mary has chosen that good part, which will not be taken away from her."

love your neighbor

The parable of the Good Samaritan does a good job of encouraging us to be helpful to strangers. But sometimes I wonder if it's actually easier to be a Good Samaritan to a stranger than it is to a friend or a family member. It's easier to help the guy with the flat tire on the side of the road or a bum on the street, perhaps out of pride or selfishness, just so that you can feel like you're a really good Christian—when all the time your brother or sister really needs you. I sometimes look to the street before I look right next to me—just to feel good about myself. Some of the guys in the band continually bend over backwards for me, helping me out when I need it. Then I just assume that because we're friends they're OK, and that they're getting the love that they need. Yes, it's important to reach out to strangers when we see an opportunity to show them the love of God. But there's no question that my friends also need to see the love of God shown through me—possibly even more than a stranger.

Tyler Burkum

How I'm "loving my neighbor" today:

_____

_____

_____

_____

_____

_____

_____

"You shall love the LORD your God with all your heart, with all your soul, with all your strength, and with all your mind," and "your neighbor as yourself."
(Luke 10:27b)

47

THE BEATITUDES

¹And seeing the multitudes, He went up on a mountain, and when He was seated His disciples came to Him. ²Then He opened His mouth and taught them, saying:

³ "Blessed *are* the poor in spirit,
For theirs is the kingdom of
heaven.
⁴ Blessed *are* those who mourn,
For they shall be comforted.
⁵ Blessed *are* the meek,
For they shall inherit the earth.
⁶ Blessed *are* those who hunger and
thirst for righteousness,
For they shall be filled.
⁷ Blessed *are* the merciful,
For they shall obtain mercy.
⁸ Blessed *are* the pure in heart,
For they shall see God.
⁹ Blessed *are* the peacemakers,
For they shall be called sons of
God.
¹⁰ Blessed *are* those who are
persecuted for righteousness'
sake,
For theirs is the kingdom of
heaven.

¹¹"Blessed are you when they revile and persecute you, and say all kinds of evil against you falsely for My sake. ¹²Rejoice and be exceedingly glad, for great *is* your reward in heaven, for so they persecuted the prophets who were before you.

BELIEVERS ARE SALT AND LIGHT

¹³"You are the salt of the earth; but if the salt loses its flavor, how shall it be seasoned? It is then good for nothing but to be thrown out and trampled underfoot by men.

¹⁴"You are the light of the world. A city that is set on a hill cannot be hidden. ¹⁵Nor do they light a lamp and put it under a basket, but on a lampstand, and it gives light to all *who are* in the house. ¹⁶Let your light so shine before men, that they may see your good works and glorify your Father in heaven.

CHRIST FULFILLS THE LAW

¹⁷"Do not think that I came to destroy the Law or the Prophets. I did not come to destroy but to fulfill. ¹⁸For assuredly, I say to you, till heaven and earth pass away, one jot or one tittle will by no means pass from the law till all is fulfilled. ¹⁹Whoever therefore breaks one of the least of these commandments, and teaches men so, shall be called least in the kingdom of heaven; but whoever does and teaches *them*, he shall be called great in the kingdom of heaven. ²⁰For I say to you, that unless your righteousness exceeds *the righteousness* of the scribes and Pharisees, you will by no means enter the kingdom of heaven.

MURDER BEGINS IN THE HEART

²¹"You have heard that it was said to those of old, 'You shall not murder, and whoever murders will be in danger of the judgment.' ²²But I say to you that whoever is angry with his brother without a cause shall be in danger of the judgment. And whoever says to his brother, 'Raca!' shall be in danger of the council. But whoever says, 'You fool!' shall be in danger of hell fire. ²³Therefore if you bring your gift to the altar, and there remember that your brother has

something against you, [24]leave your gift there before the altar, and go your way. First be reconciled to your brother, and then come and offer your gift. [25]Agree with your adversary quickly, while you are on the way with him, lest your adversary deliver you to the judge, the judge hand you over to the officer, and you be thrown into prison. [26]Assuredly, I say to you, you will by no means get out of there till you have paid the last penny.

ADULTERY IN THE HEART

[27]"You have heard that it was said to those of old, 'You shall not commit adultery.' [28]But I say to you that whoever looks at a woman to lust for her has already committed adultery with her in his heart. [29]If your right eye causes you to sin, pluck it out and cast *it* from you; for it is more profitable for you that one of your members perish, than for your whole body to be cast into hell. [30]And if your right hand causes you to sin, cut it off and cast *it* from you; for it is more profitable for you that one of your members perish, than for your whole body to be cast into hell.

MARRIAGE IS SACRED AND BINDING

[31]"Furthermore it has been said, 'Whoever divorces his wife, let him give her a certificate of divorce.' [32]But I say to you that whoever divorces his wife for any reason except sexual immorality causes her to commit adultery; and whoever marries a woman who is divorced commits adultery.

JESUS FORBIDS OATHS

[33]"Again you have heard that it was said to those of old, 'You shall not swear falsely, but shall perform your oaths to the Lord.' [34]But I say to you, do not swear at all: neither by heaven, for it is God's throne; [35]nor by the earth, for it is His footstool; nor by Jerusalem, for it is the city of the great King. [36]Nor shall you swear by your head, because you cannot make one hair white or black. [37]But let your 'Yes' be 'Yes,' and your 'No,' 'No.' For whatever is more than these is from the evil one.

GO THE SECOND MILE

[38]"You have heard that it was said, 'An eye for an eye and a tooth for a tooth.' [39]But I tell you not to resist an evil person. But whoever slaps you on your right cheek, turn the other to him also. [40]If anyone wants to sue you and take away your tunic, let him have *your* cloak also. [41]And whoever compels you to go one mile, go with him two. [42]Give to him who asks you, and from him who wants to borrow from you do not turn away.

LOVE YOUR ENEMIES

[43]"You have heard that it was said, 'You shall love your neighbor and hate your enemy.' [44]But I say to you, love your enemies, bless those who curse you, do good to those who hate you, and pray for those who spitefully use you and persecute you, [45]that you may be sons of your Father in heaven; for He makes His sun rise on the evil and on the good, and sends rain on the just and on the unjust. [46]For if you love those who love you, what reward have you? Do not even the tax collectors do the same? [47]And if you greet your brethren only, what do you do more *than others*? Do not even the tax collectors do so? [48]Therefore you shall be perfect, just as your Father in heaven is perfect.

blessed are you

Every time I read the Beatitudes they point out to me how they are the complete opposite of what the world thinks. I find it so easy to get sucked into the world. Most of the time I'm living the opposite of what I know I'm supposed to be living. "Blessed are the meek" probably hits me the hardest. We don't approach AA as great musicians, but rather as people who just want to serve God, and He has blessed that. But getting the attitude of brokenness when you're continually on stage is really hard. When people are catering to me or applauding me, I want to remain broken before God. I do that by getting in the Word and reading scriptures that cut to the core of who I am. God doesn't allow us to become too haughty. Just when we think we're doing great and things are really moving up, we'll get hit by something that will keep us completely dependent on God and not ourselves. He will give us favor, but it won't come through us. It's in seeking God in His Word. Then God can step in and shut us down.

Mark Stuart

How I'm becoming broken before God:

_____

_____

_____

_____

_____

_____

_____

_____

Blessed are the meek, for they
shall inherit the earth.
(Matthew 5:5)

DO GOOD TO PLEASE GOD

[1]"Take heed that you do not do your charitable deeds before men, to be seen by them. Otherwise you have no reward from your Father in heaven. [2]Therefore, when you do a charitable deed, do not sound a trumpet before you as the hypocrites do in the synagogues and in the streets, that they may have glory from men. Assuredly, I say to you, they have their reward. [3]But when you do a charitable deed, do not let your left hand know what your right hand is doing, [4]that your charitable deed may be in secret; and your Father who sees in secret will Himself reward you openly.

THE MODEL PRAYER

[5]"And when you pray, you shall not be like the hypocrites. For they love to pray standing in the synagogues and on the corners of the streets, that they may be seen by men. Assuredly, I say to you, they have their reward. [6]But you, when you pray, go into your room, and when you have shut your door, pray to your Father who *is* in the secret *place*; and your Father who sees in secret will reward you openly. [7]And when you pray, do not use vain repetitions as the heathen *do*. For they think that they will be heard for their many words. [8]"Therefore do not be like them. For your Father knows the things you have need of before you ask Him. [9]In this manner, therefore, pray:

Our Father in heaven,
Hallowed be Your name.
[10]Your kingdom come.
Your will be done
On earth as *it is* in heaven.
[11]Give us this day our daily bread.
[12]And forgive us our debts,
As we forgive our debtors.
[13]And do not lead us into temptation,
But deliver us from the evil one.
For Yours is the kingdom and the power and the glory forever.
Amen.

[14]"For if you forgive men their trespasses, your heavenly Father will also forgive you. [15]But if you do not forgive men their trespasses, neither will your Father forgive your trespasses.

FASTING TO BE SEEN ONLY BY GOD

[16]"Moreover, when you fast, do not be like the hypocrites, with a sad countenance. For they disfigure their faces that they may appear to men to be fasting. Assuredly, I say to you, they have their reward. [17]But you, when you fast, anoint your head and wash your face, [18]so that you do not appear to men to be fasting, but to your Father who *is* in the secret *place*; and your Father who sees in secret will reward you openly.

LAY UP TREASURES IN HEAVEN

[19]"Do not lay up for yourselves treasures on earth, where moth and rust destroy and where thieves break in and steal; [20]but lay up for yourselves treasures in heaven, where neither moth nor rust destroys and where thieves do not break in and steal. [21]For where your treasure is, there your heart will be also.

THE LAMP OF THE BODY

22"The lamp of the body is the eye. If therefore your eye is good, your whole body will be full of light. 23But if your eye is bad, your whole body will be full of darkness. If therefore the light that is in you is darkness, how great *is* that darkness!

YOU CANNOT SERVE GOD AND RICHES

24"No one can serve two masters; for either he will hate the one and love the other, or else he will be loyal to the one and despise the other. You cannot serve God and mammon.

DO NOT WORRY

25"Therefore I say to you, do not worry about your life, what you will eat or what you will drink; nor about your body, what you will put on. Is not life more than food and the body more than clothing? 26Look at the birds of the air, for they neither sow nor reap nor gather into barns; yet your heavenly Father feeds them. Are you not of more value than they? 27Which of you by worrying can add one cubit to his stature?

28"So why do you worry about clothing? Consider the lilies of the field, how they grow: they neither toil nor spin; 29and yet I say to you that even Solomon in all his glory was not arrayed like one of these. 30Now if God so clothes the grass of the field, which today is, and tomorrow is thrown into the oven, *will He* not much more *clothe* you, O you of little faith?

31"Therefore do not worry, saying, 'What shall we eat?' or 'What shall we drink?' or 'What shall we wear?' 32For after all these things the Gentiles seek. For your heavenly Father knows that you need all these things. 33But seek first the kingdom of God and His righteousness, and all these things shall be added to you. 34Therefore do not worry about tomorrow, for to–morrow will worry about its own things. Sufficient for the day *is* its own trouble.

charitable deeds

DAY 14

Sometimes it's weird enough to get paid to play music, but to mix that with God and ministry—it can get pretty wacky. It's hard to not let my ministry be just a job. It's especially hard that sometimes the good things we do for people are so visible. This seems to run directly against Matthew 6:1-4. I need to strive for a relationship with God that has noth-ing to do with what other people think, and not allow the good I might do to affect how I think God looks at me. Sometimes churches can turn into a

continued on next page

show-and-tell about all the good things you are doing for other people. But instead of judging people when you see them doing things to get attention, look at the good that God can still do. He works through hypocrites and sinners all the time. God doesn't need perfect people to accomplish His will. What if you began to lead a radical revolution of silent service to the people around you? Can you get creative and start doing things for people that nobody sees you do?

Tyler Burkum

What Jesus is showing me to do for others today:

_____

_____

_____

_____

_____

_____

_____

_____

_____

_____

_____

_____

_____

_____

_____

When you do a charitable deed, do not let your left hand know what your right hand is doing. (Matthew 6:3)

DO NOT JUDGE

[1]"Judge not, that you be not judged. [2]For with what judgment you judge, you will be judged; and with the measure you use, it will be measured back to you. [3]And why do you look at the speck in your brother's eye, but do not consider the plank in your own eye? [4]Or how can you say to your brother, 'Let me remove the speck from your eye'; and look, a plank is in your own eye? [5]Hypocrite! First remove the plank from your own eye, and then you will see clearly to remove the speck from your brother's eye.

[6]"Do not give what is holy to the dogs; nor cast your pearls before swine, lest they trample them under their feet, and turn and tear you in pieces.

KEEP ASKING, SEEKING, KNOCKING

[7]"Ask, and it will be given to you; seek, and you will find; knock, and it will be opened to you. [8]For everyone who asks receives, and he who seeks finds, and to him who knocks it will be opened. [9]Or what man is there among you who, if his son asks for bread, will give him a stone? [10]Or if he asks for a fish, will he give him a serpent? [11]If you then, being evil, know how to give good gifts to your children, how much more will your Father who is in heaven give good things to those who ask Him! [12]Therefore, whatever you want men to do to you, do also to them, for this is the Law and the Prophets.

THE NARROW WAY

[13]"Enter by the narrow gate; for wide is the gate and broad is the way that leads to destruction, and there are many who go in by it. [14]Because narrow is the gate and difficult is the way which leads to life, and there are few who find it.

YOU WILL KNOW THEM BY THEIR FRUITS

[15]"Beware of false prophets, who come to you in sheep's clothing, but inwardly they are ravenous wolves. [16]You will know them by their fruits. Do men gather grapes from thorn-bushes or figs from thistles? [17]Even so, every good tree bears good fruit, but a bad tree bears bad fruit. [18]A good tree cannot bear bad fruit, nor can a bad tree bear good fruit. [19]Every tree that does not bear good fruit is cut down and thrown into the fire. [20]Therefore by their fruits you will know them.

I NEVER KNEW YOU

[21]"Not everyone who says to Me, 'Lord, Lord,' shall enter the kingdom of heaven, but he who does the will of My Father in heaven. [22]Many will say to Me in that day, 'Lord, Lord, have we not prophesied in Your name, cast out demons in Your name, and done many wonders in Your name?' [23]And then I will declare to them, 'I never knew you; depart from Me, you who practice lawlessness!'

BUILD ON THE ROCK

[24]"Therefore whoever hears these sayings of Mine, and does them, I will liken him to a wise man who built his house on the rock: [25]and the rain descended, the floods came, and the winds blew and beat on that house;

and it did not fall, for it was founded on the rock. ²⁶"But everyone who hears these sayings of Mine, and does not do them, will be like a foolish man who built his house on the sand: ²⁷and the rain descended, the floods came, and the winds blew and beat on that house; and it fell. And great was its fall."

²⁸And so it was, when Jesus had ended these sayings, that the people were astonished at His teaching, ²⁹for He taught them as one having authority, and not as the scribes.

judging others

The Bible is pretty clear that we're not supposed to judge, unless we ourselves want to be judged. Who wants that? I guess I do, since judging is a big thing for me. I hate that I do it, but I find it pretty easy a lot of times. It's especially easy to judge other Christian people, probably because I can focus so much on all the things I think I'm supposed to be doing, giving me a right to expect others to do those things as well. Usually, though, I find myself judging someone for doing something that I just did an hour ago! I have to keep reminding myself that I have no right to judge other people since I can never know what they might be going through. It's also important for me to keep seeking God, because the truth of God exposes the sin in my own life. The awareness of this sin keeps me on my knees, and in constant need of God's grace and mercy. I believe that's what other people deserve from me as well.

Ben Cissell

What Jesus is telling me about judging others:

_____

_____

_____

_____

_____

_____

_____

_____

_____

_____

_____

_____

_____

_____

_____

_____

_____

_____

_____

_____

> "Judge not, that you be not judged. For with what judgment you judge, you will be judged." (Matthew 7:1, 2a)

A MAN WITH DROPSY HEALED ON THE SABBATH

¹Now it happened, as He went into the house of one of the rulers of the Pharisees to eat bread on the Sabbath, that they watched Him closely. ²And behold, there was a certain man before Him who had dropsy. ³And Jesus, answering, spoke to the lawyers and Pharisees, saying, "Is it lawful to heal on the Sabbath?"

⁴But they kept silent. And He took *him* and healed him, and let him go. ⁵Then He answered them, saying, "Which of you, having a donkey or an ox that has fallen into a pit, will not immediately pull him out on the Sabbath day?" ⁶And they could not answer Him regarding these things.

TAKE THE LOWLY PLACE

⁷So He told a parable to those who were invited, when He noted how they chose the best places, saying to them: ⁸"When you are invited by anyone to a wedding feast, do not sit down in the best place, lest one more honorable than you be invited by him; ⁹and he who invited you and him come and say to you, 'Give place to this man,' and then you begin with shame to take the lowest place. ¹⁰But when you are invited, go and sit down in the lowest place, so that when he who invited you comes he may say to you, 'Friend, go up higher.' Then you will have glory in the presence of those who sit at the table with you. ¹¹For whoever exalts himself will be humbled, and he who humbles himself will be exalted."

¹²Then He also said to him who invited Him, "When you give a dinner or a supper, do not ask your friends, your brothers, your relatives, nor rich neighbors, lest they also invite you back, and you be repaid. ¹³But when you give a feast, invite *the* poor, *the* maimed, *the* lame, *the* blind. ¹⁴And you will be blessed, because they cannot repay you; for you shall be repaid at the resurrection of the just."

THE PARABLE OF THE GREAT SUPPER

¹⁵Now when one of those who sat at the table with Him heard these things, he said to Him, "Blessed *is* he who shall eat bread in the kingdom of God!"

¹⁶Then He said to him, "A certain man gave a great supper and invited many, ¹⁷and sent his servant at supper time to say to those who were invited, 'Come, for all things are now ready.' ¹⁸But they all with one *accord* began to make excuses. The first said to him, 'I have bought a piece of ground, and I must go and see it. I ask you to have me excused.' ¹⁹And another said, 'I have bought five yoke of oxen, and I am going to test them. I ask you to have me excused.' ²⁰Still another said, 'I have married a wife, and therefore I cannot come.' ²¹So that servant came and reported these things to his master. Then the master of the house, being angry, said to his servant, 'Go out quickly into the streets and lanes of the city, and bring in here *the* poor and *the* maimed and *the* lame and *the* blind.' ²²And the servant said, 'Master, it is done as you commanded, and still there is room.' ²³Then the master said to the servant, 'Go out into the highways and hedges, and compel *them* to come in, that my house may be filled. ²⁴For I say to you that none of those

men who were invited shall taste my supper.' "

LEAVING ALL TO FOLLOW CHRIST

25Now great multitudes went with Him. And He turned and said to them, 26"If anyone comes to Me and does not hate his father and mother, wife and children, brothers and sisters, yes, and his own life also, he cannot be My disciple. 27And whoever does not bear his cross and come after Me cannot be My disciple. 28For which of you, intending to build a tower, does not sit down first and count the cost, whether he has *enough* to finish *it*— 29lest, after he has laid the foundation, and is not able to finish, all who see *it* begin to mock him,

30saying, 'This man began to build and was not able to finish.' 31Or what king, going to make war against another king, does not sit down first and consider whether he is able with ten thousand to meet him who comes against him with twenty thousand? 32Or else, while the other is still a great way off, he sends a delegation and asks conditions of peace. 33So likewise, whoever of you does not forsake all that he has cannot be My disciple.

TASTELESS SALT IS WORTHLESS

34"Salt *is* good; but if the salt has lost its flavor, how shall it be seasoned? 35It is neither fit for the land nor for the dunghill, *but* men throw it out. He who has ears to hear, let him hear!"

radical discipleship

Jesus always talked about our need to give up everything in order to follow Him. This isn't too difficult when you don't own many things, except maybe a beat-up car and a bunch of CDs. But I've got to believe He means that we have to be willing to let go of everything we're holding onto in our hearts as well. I might have some great goals or dreams I'm convinced God needs to make happen. Maybe it's a certain habit or a relationship God is trying to tell me to remove from my life. I have to be willing to let go of anything I'm holding onto in order to be His disciple. That's why Jesus calls it a cross, because there will be some pain involved in sacrificing what might seem important to you, to accept what is important to Him! It's what is truly valuable that no man could ever take away from you. What are you holding onto too tightly that God might be asking you to let go of?

Ben Cissell

What Jesus is asking me to give up for Him:

_____

_____

_____

_____

_____

_____

_____

_____

_____

_____

_____

_____

_____

_____

_____

_____

_____

_____

_____

_____

"And whoever does not bear his cross and come after Me cannot be My disciple."
(Luke 14:27)

THE PARABLE OF THE LOST SHEEP

¹Then all the tax collectors and the sinners drew near to Him to hear Him. ²And the Pharisees and scribes complained, saying, "This Man receives sinners and eats with them." ³So He spoke this parable to them, saying:

⁴"What man of you, having a hundred sheep, if he loses one of them, does not leave the ninety-nine in the wilderness, and go after the one which is lost until he finds it? ⁵And when he has found *it*, he lays *it* on his shoulders, rejoicing. ⁶And when he comes home, he calls together *his* friends and neighbors, saying to them, 'Rejoice with me, for I have found my sheep which was lost!' ⁷I say to you that likewise there will be more joy in heaven over one sinner who repents than over ninety-nine just persons who need no repentance.

THE PARABLE OF THE LOST COIN

⁸"Or what woman, having ten silver coins, if she loses one coin, does not light a lamp, sweep the house, and search carefully until she finds *it*? ⁹And when she has found *it*, she calls *her* friends and neighbors together, saying, 'Rejoice with me, for I have found the piece which I lost!' ¹⁰Likewise, I say to you, there is joy in the presence of the angels of God over one sinner who repents."

THE PARABLE OF THE LOST SON

¹¹Then He said: "A certain man had two sons. ¹²And the younger of them said to *his* father, 'Father, give me the portion of goods that falls *to me*.' So he divided to them *his* livelihood. ¹³And not many days after, the younger son gathered all together, journeyed to a far country, and there wasted his possessions with prodigal living. ¹⁴But when he had spent all, there arose a severe famine in that land, and he began to be in want. ¹⁵Then he went and joined himself to a citizen of that country, and he sent him into his fields to feed swine. ¹⁶And he would gladly have filled his stomach with the pods that the swine ate, and no one gave him *anything*.

¹⁷"But when he came to himself, he said, 'How many of my father's hired servants have bread enough and to spare, and I perish with hunger! ¹⁸I will arise and go to my father, and will say to him, "Father, I have sinned against heaven and before you, ¹⁹and I am no longer worthy to be called your son. Make me like one of your hired servants." '

²⁰"And he arose and came to his father. But when he was still a great way off, his father saw him and had compassion, and ran and fell on his neck and kissed him. ²¹And the son said to him, 'Father, I have sinned against heaven and in your sight, and am no longer worthy to be called your son.'

²²"But the father said to his servants, 'Bring out the best robe and put *it* on him, and put a ring on his hand and sandals on *his* feet. ²³And bring the fatted calf here and kill *it*, and let us eat and be merry; ²⁴for this my son was dead and is alive again; he was lost and is found.' And they began to be merry.

25"Now his older son was in the field. And as he came and drew near to the house, he heard music and dancing. 26So he called one of the servants and asked what these things meant. 27And he said to him, 'Your brother has come, and because he has received him safe and sound, your father has killed the fatted calf.'

28"But he was angry and would not go in. Therefore his father came out and pleaded with him. 29So he answered and said to *his* father, 'Lo, these many years I have been serving you; I never transgressed your commandment at any time; and yet you never gave me a young goat, that I might make merry with my friends. 30But as soon as this son of yours came, who has devoured your livelihood with harlots, you killed the fatted calf for him.'

31"And he said to him, 'Son, you are always with me, and all that I have is yours. 32It was right that we should make merry and be glad, for your brother was dead and is alive again, and was lost and is found.' "

coming home

God's love for you is so personal. This is shown so vividly in these parables. God is constantly pursuing the lost sheep, or the lost coin, or the lost son. He puts so much value on individuals regardless of what they have done. It's so cool to think that the father who threw the huge party when his son came home didn't wait to see if he had his life all cleaned up. His son came home and that's all the father needed in order to celebrate. As the lost son or daughter, there's no need to think you have to get your life together before you can come to God. He's waiting for you to just turn to Him and come join in the party He's prepared to throw in your honor. Your own parents might be spread thin and seem too busy for you, but God is seeking out a very personal relationship with you. Some people say they can't believe in a God who runs the whole world; He probably doesn't have any time for them. It's because He is God that He does have time for you—as well as a lot of love that He is waiting to give.

Tyler Burkum

What God is telling me in His Word today:

_____

_____

_____

_____

_____

_____

_____

_____

_____

_____

_____

_____

_____

_____

_____

_____

_____

_____

_____

_____

_____

_____

"There is joy in the presence of the angels of God over one sinner who repents."
(Luke 15:10b)

THE PARABLE OF THE UNJUST STEWARD

[1]He also said to His disciples: "There was a certain rich man who had a steward, and an accusation was brought to him that this man was wasting his goods. [2]So he called him and said to him, 'What is this I hear about you? Give an account of your stewardship, for you can no longer be steward.'

[3]"Then the steward said within himself, 'What shall I do? For my master is taking the stewardship away from me. I cannot dig; I am ashamed to beg. [4]I have resolved what to do, that when I am put out of the stewardship, they may receive me into their houses.'

[5]"So he called every one of his master's debtors to *him*, and said to the first, 'How much do you owe my master?' [6]And he said, 'A hundred measures of oil.' So he said to him, 'Take your bill, and sit down quickly and write fifty.' [7]Then he said to another, 'And how much do you owe?' So he said, 'A hundred measures of wheat.' And he said to him, 'Take your bill, and write eighty.' [8]So the master commended the unjust steward because he had dealt shrewdly. For the sons of this world are more shrewd in their generation than the sons of light.

[9]"And I say to you, make friends for yourselves by unrighteous mammon, that when you fail, they may receive you into an everlasting home. [10]He who *is* faithful in *what is* least is faithful also in much; and he who is unjust in *what is* least is unjust also in much. [11]Therefore if you have not been faithful in the unrighteous mammon, who will commit to your trust the true *riches*? [12]And if you have not been faithful in what is another man's, who will give you what is your own?

[13]"No servant can serve two masters; for either he will hate the one and love the other, or else he will be loyal to the one and despise the other. You cannot serve God and mammon."

THE LAW, THE PROPHETS, AND THE KINGDOM

[14]Now the Pharisees, who were lovers of money, also heard all these things, and they derided Him. [15]And He said to them, "You are those who justify yourselves before men, but God knows your hearts. For what is highly esteemed among men is an abomination in the sight of God.

[16]"The law and the prophets *were* until John. Since that time the kingdom of God has been preached, and everyone is pressing into it. [17]And it is easier for heaven and earth to pass away than for one tittle of the law to fail.

[18]"Whoever divorces his wife and marries another commits adultery; and whoever marries her who is divorced from *her* husband commits adultery.

THE RICH MAN AND LAZARUS

[19]"There was a certain rich man who was clothed in purple and fine linen and fared sumptuously every day. [20]But there was a certain beggar named Lazarus, full of sores, who was

laid at his gate, ²¹desiring to be fed with the crumbs which fell from the rich man's table. Moreover the dogs came and licked his sores. ²²So it was that the beggar died, and was carried by the angels to Abraham's bosom. The rich man also died and was buried. ²³And being in torments in Hades, he lifted up his eyes and saw Abraham afar off, and Lazarus in his bosom.

²⁴"Then he cried and said, 'Father Abraham, have mercy on me, and send Lazarus that he may dip the tip of his finger in water and cool my tongue; for I am tormented in this flame.' ²⁵But Abraham said, 'Son, remember that in your lifetime you received your good things, and likewise Lazarus evil things; but now he is comforted and you are tormented. ²⁶And besides all this, between us and you there is a great gulf fixed, so that those who want to pass from here to you cannot, nor can those from there pass to us.'

²⁷"Then he said, 'I beg you therefore, father, that you would send him to my father's house, ²⁸for I have five brothers, that he may testify to them, lest they also come to this place of torment.' ²⁹Abraham said to him, 'They have Moses and the prophets; let them hear them.' ³⁰And he said, 'No, father Abraham; but if one goes to them from the dead, they will repent.' ³¹But he said to him, 'If they do not hear Moses and the prophets, neither will they be persuaded though one rise from the dead.' "

what really matters

The story of the rich man and Lazarus is such a huge paradox. Once again, it's a testimony to the underdog who defeats the odds and comes out on top in the end. One of the things that's hard about the music industry is that we are continually being charted, compared, and measured against all the other bands. Who is selling the most is suddenly the most valuable, and whoever is having their songs climb the highest on the radio charts is in the most demand. From a business standpoint I can see how this matters. But none of it matters in the end. John F. Kennedy, Jr. interviewed Billy Graham and asked him what had been the biggest surprise in his life. Graham answered, "The brevity of life." We strive to be-

continued on next page

come wealthy and comfortable. We even strive to be noticed and deemed important by other men. I love having a top-selling album or a number one song. But I can't forget that God is most concerned about whether or not we're going to spend eternity with Him.

Mark Stuart

How I'm getting more extreme for Jesus today:

So it was that the beggar died, and was carried by the angels to Abraham's bosom.
(Luke 16:22a)

AN ADULTERESS FACES THE LIGHT OF THE WORLD

[1]But Jesus went to the Mount of Olives.

[2]Now early in the morning He came again into the temple, and all the people came to Him; and He sat down and taught them. [3]Then the scribes and Pharisees brought to Him a woman caught in adultery. And when they had set her in the midst, [4]they said to Him, "Teacher, this woman was caught in adultery, in the very act. [5]Now Moses, in the law, commanded us that such should be stoned. But what do You say?" [6]This they said, testing Him, that they might have *something* of which to accuse Him. But Jesus stooped down and wrote on the ground with *His* finger, as though He did not hear.

[7]So when they continued asking Him, He raised Himself up and said to them, "He who is without sin among you, let him throw a stone at her first." [8]And again He stooped down and wrote on the ground. [9]Then those who heard *it*, being convicted by *their* conscience, went out one by one, beginning with the oldest *even* to the last. And Jesus was left alone, and the woman standing in the midst. [10]When Jesus had raised Himself up and saw no one but the woman, He said to her, "Woman, where are those accusers of yours? Has no one condemned you?"

[11]She said, "No one, Lord."

And Jesus said to her, "Neither do I condemn you; go and sin no more."

[12]Then Jesus spoke to them again, saying, "I am the light of the world. He who follows Me shall not walk in darkness, but have the light of life."

JESUS DEFENDS HIS SELF-WITNESS

[13]The Pharisees therefore said to Him, "You bear witness of Yourself; Your witness is not true."

[14]Jesus answered and said to them, "Even if I bear witness of Myself, My witness is true, for I know where I came from and where I am going; but you do not know where I come from and where I am going. [15]You judge according to the flesh; I judge no one. [16]And yet if I do judge, My judgment is true; for I am not alone, but I *am* with the Father who sent Me. [17]It is also written in your law that the testimony of two men is true. [18]I am One who bears witness of Myself, and the Father who sent Me bears witness of Me."

[19]Then they said to Him, "Where is Your Father?"

Jesus answered, "You know neither Me nor My Father. If you had known Me, you would have known My Father also."

[20]These words Jesus spoke in the treasury, as He taught in the temple; and no one laid hands on Him, for His hour had not yet come.

JESUS PREDICTS HIS DEPARTURE

[21]Then Jesus said to them again, "I am going away, and you will seek Me, and will die in your sin. Where I go you cannot come."

[22]So the Jews said, "Will He kill Himself, because He says, 'Where I go you cannot come'?"

[23]And He said to them, "You are from beneath; I am from above. You are of

this world; I am not of this world. [24]Therefore I said to you that you will die in your sins; for if you do not believe that I am *He*, you will die in your sins."

[25]Then they said to Him, "Who are You?"

And Jesus said to them, "Just what I have been saying to you from the beginning. [26]I have many things to say and to judge concerning you, but He who sent Me is true; and I speak to the world those things which I heard from Him."

[27]They did not understand that He spoke to them of the Father.

[28]Then Jesus said to them, "When you lift up the Son of Man, then you will know that I am *He*, and *that* I do nothing of Myself; but as My Father taught Me, I speak these things. [29]And He who sent Me is with Me. The Father has not left Me alone, for I always do those things that please Him." [30]As He spoke these words, many believed in Him.

THE TRUTH SHALL MAKE YOU FREE

[31]Then Jesus said to those Jews who believed Him, "If you abide in My word, you are My disciples indeed. [32]And you shall know the truth, and the truth shall make you free."

[33]They answered Him, "We are Abraham's descendants, and have never been in bondage to anyone. How *can* You say, 'You will be made free'?"

[34]Jesus answered them, "Most assuredly, I say to you, whoever commits sin is a slave of sin. [35]And a slave does not abide in the house forever, *but* a son abides forever. [36]Therefore if the Son makes you free, you shall be free indeed.

ABRAHAM'S SEED AND SATAN'S

[37]"I know that you are Abraham's descendants, but you seek to kill Me, because My word has no place in you. [38]I speak what I have seen with My Father, and you do what you have seen with your father."

[39]They answered and said to Him, "Abraham is our father."

Jesus said to them, "If you were Abraham's children, you would do the works of Abraham. [40]But now you seek to kill Me, a Man who has told you the truth which I heard from God. Abraham did not do this. [41]You do the deeds of your father."

Then they said to Him, "We were not born of fornication; we have one Father—God."

[42]Jesus said to them, "If God were your Father, you would love Me, for I proceeded forth and came from God; nor have I come of Myself, but He sent Me. [43]Why do you not understand My speech? Because you are not able to listen to My word. [44]You are of *your* father the devil, and the desires of your father you want to do. He was a murderer from the beginning, and does not stand in the truth, because there is no truth in him. When he speaks a lie, he speaks from his own *resources*, for he is a liar and the father of it. [45]But because I tell the truth, you do not believe Me. [46]Which of you convicts Me of sin? And if I tell the truth, why do you not believe Me? [47]He who is of God hears God's words; therefore you do not hear, because you are not of God."

BEFORE ABRAHAM WAS, I AM

[48]Then the Jews answered and said to Him, "Do we not say rightly that You are a Samaritan and have a demon?"

[49]Jesus answered, "I do not have a demon; but I honor My Father, and you dishonor Me. [50]And I do not seek

My *own* glory; there is One who seeks and judges. [51]Most assuredly, I say to you, if anyone keeps My word he shall never see death."

[52]Then the Jews said to Him, "Now we know that You have a demon! Abraham is dead, and the prophets; and You say, 'If anyone keeps My word he shall never taste death.' [53]Are You greater than our father Abraham, who is dead? And the prophets are dead. Who do You make Yourself out to be?"

[54]Jesus answered, "If I honor Myself, My honor is nothing. It is My Father who honors Me, of whom you say that He is your God. [55]Yet you have not known Him, but I know Him. And if I say, 'I do not know Him,' I shall be a liar like you; but I do know Him and keep His word. [56]Your father Abraham rejoiced to see My day, and he saw *it* and was glad."

[57]Then the Jews said to Him, "You are not yet fifty years old, and have You seen Abraham?"

[58]Jesus said to them, "Most as–suredly, I say to you, before Abraham was, I AM."

[59]Then they took up stones to throw at Him; but Jesus hid Himself and went out of the temple, going through the midst of them, and so passed by.

loving instead of judging

The scribes and Pharisees were trying to corner Jesus into saying something bad about the adulteress, but He didn't. Why do I find it so easy? I walked into a store the other day and immediately noticed that one of the clerks appeared to be a homosexual. I judged him even before I talked to him. He asked me what I did, and I told him I was a drummer. Then he asked for whom, and I told him Audio Adrenaline. He then started off on me about Christians and how closed-minded and judgmental they are. He was convinced that I couldn't like him because of his experience of being judged by others. I started to get a little mad about how he immediately judged me as being a certain way because of some bad experience he had with Christians sometime in his life. Then I remembered how I was just as quick to judge him. Instead of judging I must choose to love people who might be different from me. I must never forget that God doesn't have an ounce more of love for me than he does for that guy.

Ben Cissell

How I'm allowing God's love to speak through me today:

Jesus said to her, "Neither do I condemn you; go and sin no more." (John 8:11b)

day 20

JESUS WARNS OF OFFENSES

¹Then He said to the disciples, "It is impossible that no offenses should come, but woe *to him* through whom they do come! ²It would be better for him if a millstone were hung around his neck, and he were thrown into the sea, than that he should offend one of these little ones. ³Take heed to yourselves. If your brother sins against you, rebuke him; and if he repents, forgive him. ⁴And if he sins against you seven times in a day, and seven times in a day returns to you, saying, 'I repent,' you shall forgive him."

FAITH AND DUTY

⁵And the apostles said to the Lord, "Increase our faith."

⁶So the Lord said, "If you have faith as a mustard seed, you can say to this mulberry tree, 'Be pulled up by the roots and be planted in the sea,' and it would obey you. ⁷And which of you, having a servant plowing or tending sheep, will say to him when he has come in from the field, 'Come at once and sit down to eat'? ⁸But will he not rather say to him, 'Prepare something for my supper, and gird yourself and serve me till I have eaten and drunk, and afterward you will eat and drink'? ⁹Does he thank that servant because he did the things that were commanded him? I think not. ¹⁰So likewise you, when you have done all those things which you are commanded, say, 'We are unprofitable servants. We have done what was our duty to do.' "

TEN LEPERS CLEANSED

¹¹Now it happened as He went to Jerusalem that He passed through the midst of Samaria and Galilee. ¹²Then as He entered a certain village, there met Him ten men who were lepers, who stood afar off. ¹³And they lifted up *their* voices and said, "Jesus, Master, have mercy on us!"

¹⁴So when He saw *them*, He said to them, "Go, show yourselves to the priests." And so it was that as they went, they were cleansed.

¹⁵And one of them, when he saw that he was healed, returned, and with a loud voice glorified God, ¹⁶and fell down on *his* face at His feet, giving Him thanks. And he was a Samaritan.

¹⁷So Jesus answered and said, "Were there not ten cleansed? But where *are* the nine? ¹⁸Were there not any found who returned to give glory to God except this foreigner?" ¹⁹And He said to him, "Arise, go your way. Your faith has made you well."

THE COMING OF THE KINGDOM

²⁰Now when He was asked by the Pharisees when the kingdom of God would come, He answered them and said, "The kingdom of God does not come with observation; ²¹nor will they say, 'See here!' or 'See there!' For indeed, the kingdom of God is within you."

²²Then He said to the disciples, "The days will come when you will desire to see one of the days of the Son of Man, and you will not see *it*. ²³And they will say to you, 'Look here!' or

73

'Look there!' Do not go after *them* or follow *them*. ²⁴For as the lightning that flashes out of one *part* under heaven shines to the other *part* under heaven, so also the Son of Man will be in His day. ²⁵But first He must suffer many things and be rejected by this generation. ²⁶And as it was in the days of Noah, so it will be also in the days of the Son of Man: ²⁷They ate, they drank, they married wives, they were given in marriage, until the day that Noah entered the ark, and the flood came and destroyed them all. ²⁸Likewise as it was also in the days of Lot: They ate, they drank, they bought, they sold, they planted, they built; ²⁹but on the day that Lot went out of Sodom it rained fire and brimstone from heaven and destroyed *them* all. ³⁰Even so will it be in the day when the Son of Man is revealed.

³¹"In that day, he who is on the housetop, and his goods *are* in the house, let him not come down to take them away. And likewise the one who is in the field, let him not turn back. ³²Remember Lot's wife. ³³Whoever seeks to save his life will lose it, and whoever loses his life will preserve it. ³⁴I tell you, in that night there will be two *men* in one bed: the one will be taken and the other will be left. ³⁵Two *women* will be grinding together: the one will be taken and the other left. ³⁶Two *men* will be in the field: the one will be taken and the other left."

³⁷And they answered and said to Him, "Where, Lord?"

So He said to them, "Wherever the body is, there the eagles will be gathered together."

thanks be to God!

DAY 20

When I was 17 my family moved to Haiti. Believe it or not, I saw a lot of leprosy, just like is mentioned in the Bible. What amazed me was how people with this disease were shunned, very much similar to people with AIDS. Jesus didn't ask the ten lepers, "OK, what did you do to get this disease?" He healed them regardless of what brought them to their place of disease. Even today He does the same for us. Regardless of what we've done in our lives, He sees our sin disease and tells us that we can be healed. How interesting it is in this story that only one guy came

continued on next page

back and thanked Him! What happened to the other nine? I find it so easy to take for granted the things that Christ has done for me. It especially hits me when I think about what my life would be like without having received the healing from my sin. Would you be the one who came back to thank Jesus, or would you be off with the other nine who were healed, but had lost sight of the Source of their healing?

Mark Stuart

• • • ● • • •

How I'm showing my thanks to God today:

_____

_____

_____

_____

_____

_____

_____

_____

_____

_____

_____

_____

_____

_____

_____

One of them, when he saw that he was healed, returned, and with a loud voice glorified God . . . giving Him thanks.
(Luke 17:15, 16a)

THE PARABLE OF THE PERSISTENT WIDOW

[1]Then He spoke a parable to them, that men always ought to pray and not lose heart, [2]saying: "There was in a certain city a judge who did not fear God nor regard man. [3]Now there was a widow in that city; and she came to him, saying, 'Get justice for me from my adversary.' [4]And he would not for a while; but afterward he said within himself, 'Though I do not fear God nor regard man, [5]yet because this widow troubles me I will avenge her, lest by her continual coming she weary me.' "

[6]Then the Lord said, "Hear what the unjust judge said. [7]And shall God not avenge His own elect who cry out day and night to Him, though He bears long with them? [8]I tell you that He will avenge them speedily. Nevertheless, when the Son of Man comes, will He really find faith on the earth?"

THE PARABLE OF THE PHARISEE AND THE TAX COLLECTOR

[9]Also He spoke this parable to some who trusted in themselves that they were righteous, and despised others: [10]"Two men went up to the temple to pray, one a Pharisee and the other a tax collector. [11]The Pharisee stood and prayed thus with himself, 'God, I thank You that I am not like other men—extortioners, unjust, adulterers, or even as this tax collector. [12]I fast twice a week; I give tithes of all that I possess.' [13]And the tax collector, standing afar off, would not so much as raise *his* eyes to heaven, but beat his breast, saying, 'God, be merciful to me a sinner!' [14]I tell you, this man

went down to his house justified *rather* than the other; for everyone who exalts himself will be humbled, and he who humbles himself will be exalted."

JESUS BLESSES LITTLE CHILDREN

[15]Then they also brought infants to Him that He might touch them; but when the disciples saw *it*, they rebuked them. [16]But Jesus called them to *Him* and said, "Let the little children come to Me, and do not forbid them; for of such is the kingdom of God. [17]Assuredly, I say to you, whoever does not receive the kingdom of God as a little child will by no means enter it."

JESUS COUNSELS THE RICH YOUNG RULER

[18]Now a certain ruler asked Him, saying, "Good Teacher, what shall I do to inherit eternal life?"

[19]So Jesus said to him, "Why do you call Me good? No one *is* good but One, *that is*, God. [20]You know the commandments: 'Do not commit adultery,' 'Do not murder,' 'Do not steal,' 'Do not bear false witness,' 'Honor your father and your mother.' "

[21]And he said, "All these things I have kept from my youth."

[22]So when Jesus heard these things, He said to him, "You still lack one thing. Sell all that you have and distribute to the poor, and you will have treasure in heaven; and come, follow Me."

[23]But when he heard this, he became very sorrowful, for he was very rich.

WITH GOD ALL THINGS ARE POSSIBLE

²⁴And when Jesus saw that he became very sorrowful, He said, "How hard it is for those who have riches to enter the kingdom of God! ²⁵For it is easier for a camel to go through the eye of a needle than for a rich man to enter the kingdom of God."

²⁶And those who heard it said, "Who then can be saved?"

²⁷But He said, "The things which are impossible with men are possible with God."

²⁸Then Peter said, "See, we have left all and followed You."

²⁹So He said to them, "Assuredly, I say to you, there is no one who has left house or parents or brothers or wife or children, for the sake of the kingdom of God, ³⁰who shall not receive many times more in this present time, and in the age to come eternal life."

JESUS A THIRD TIME PREDICTS HIS DEATH AND RESURRECTION

³¹Then He took the twelve aside and said to them, "Behold, we are going up to Jerusalem, and all things that are written by the prophets concerning the Son of Man will be accomplished. ³²For He will be delivered to the Gentiles and will be mocked and insulted and spit upon. ³³They will scourge *Him* and kill Him. And the third day He will rise again."

³⁴But they understood none of these things; this saying was hidden from them, and they did not know the things which were spoken.

A BLIND MAN RECEIVES HIS SIGHT

³⁵Then it happened, as He was coming near Jericho, that a certain blind man sat by the road begging. ³⁶And hearing a multitude passing by, he asked what it meant. ³⁷So they told him that Jesus of Nazareth was passing by. ³⁸And he cried out, saying, "Jesus, Son of David, have mercy on me!"

³⁹Then those who went before warned him that he should be quiet; but he cried out all the more, "Son of David, have mercy on me!"

⁴⁰So Jesus stood still and commanded him to be brought to Him. And when he had come near, He asked him, ⁴¹saying, "What do you want Me to do for you?"

He said, "Lord, that I may receive my sight."

⁴²Then Jesus said to him, "Receive your sight; your faith has made you well." ⁴³And immediately he received his sight, and followed Him, glorifying God. And all the people, when they saw *it*, gave praise to God.

openness and brokenness

DAY 21

I have grown up as a pastor's kid. My family was always in the spotlight. We constantly had to say and do the right thing. We learned all the right words to say, and the right things to do to keep people im-

continued on next page

pressed. I'm learning now that the best thing for any leader (or really any-body) to do is to be real. Sharing your heart honestly—not saying lofty things, but revealing yourself—is the most effective way to communicate with people. Even in your talking with God, He longs for honesty. He desires for us to be completely open with Him. God would rather hear the cry of a broken heart than any lofty words. This is not about feeling guilty, but rather understanding your position before God, repenting of your sin, and believing for His forgiveness. That's when God can do the most work. This is a never-ending struggle for me. I can say all the right things when I have a microphone in my hand. But when I am humbled and broken before an audience, as well as God, that's when He will bless me and lift me up.

Mark Stuart

What God is telling me about brokenness:

_____

_____

_____

_____

_____

_____

_____

_____

_____

_____

_____

_____

A MAN BORN BLIND RECEIVES SIGHT

[1]Now as *Jesus* passed by, He saw a man who was blind from birth. [2]And His disciples asked Him, saying, "Rabbi, who sinned, this man or his parents, that he was born blind?"

[3]Jesus answered, "Neither this man nor his parents sinned, but that the works of God should be revealed in him. [4]I must work the works of Him who sent Me while it is day; *the* night is coming when no one can work. [5]As long as I am in the world, I am the light of the world."

[6]When He had said these things, He spat on the ground and made clay with the saliva; and He anointed the eyes of the blind man with the clay. [7]And He said to him, "Go, wash in the pool of Siloam" (which is translated, Sent). So he went and washed, and came back seeing.

[8]Therefore the neighbors and those who previously had seen that he was blind said, "Is not this he who sat and begged?"

[9]Some said, "This is he." Others *said,* "He is like him."

He said, "I am *he.*"

[10]Therefore they said to him, "How were your eyes opened?"

[11]He answered and said, "A Man called Jesus made clay and anointed my eyes and said to me, 'Go to the pool of Siloam and wash.' So I went and washed, and I received sight."

[12]Then they said to him, "Where is He?"

He said, "I do not know."

THE PHARISEES EXCOMMUNICATE THE HEALED MAN

[13]They brought him who formerly was blind to the Pharisees. [14]Now it was a Sabbath when Jesus made the clay and opened his eyes. [15]Then the Pharisees also asked him again how he had received his sight. He said to them, "He put clay on my eyes, and I washed, and I see."

[16]Therefore some of the Pharisees said, "This Man is not from God, because He does not keep the Sabbath."

Others said, "How can a man who is a sinner do such signs?" And there was a division among them.

[17]They said to the blind man again, "What do you say about Him because He opened your eyes?"

He said, "He is a prophet."

[18]But the Jews did not believe concerning him, that he had been blind and received his sight, until they called the parents of him who had received his sight. [19]And they asked them, saying, "Is this your son, who you say was born blind? How then does he now see?"

[20]His parents answered them and said, "We know that this is our son, and that he was born blind; [21]but by what means he now sees we do not know, or who opened his eyes we do not know. He is of age; ask him. He will speak for himself." [22]His parents said these *things* because they feared the Jews, for the Jews had agreed already that if anyone confessed *that* He *was* Christ, he would be put out of the

synagogue. [23]Therefore his parents said, "He is of age; ask him."

[24]So they again called the man who was blind, and said to him, "Give God the glory! We know that this Man is a sinner."

[25]He answered and said, "Whether He is a sinner *or not* I do not know. One thing I know: that though I was blind, now I see."

[26]Then they said to him again, "What did He do to you? How did He open your eyes?"

[27]He answered them, "I told you already, and you did not listen. Why do you want to hear *it* again? Do you also want to become His disciples?"

[28]Then they reviled him and said, "You are His disciple, but we are Moses' disciples. [29]We know that God spoke to Moses; *as for* this *fellow,* we do not know where He is from."

[30]The man answered and said to them, "Why, this is a marvelous thing, that you do not know where He is from; yet He has opened my eyes! [31]Now we know that God does not hear sinners; but if anyone is a worshiper of God and does His will, He hears him. [32]Since the world began it has been unheard of that anyone

opened the eyes of one who was born blind. [33]If this Man were not from God, He could do nothing."

[34]They answered and said to him, "You were completely born in sins, and are you teaching us?" And they cast him out.

TRUE VISION AND TRUE BLINDNESS

[35]Jesus heard that they had cast him out; and when He had found him, He said to him, "Do you believe in the Son of God?"

[36]He answered and said, "Who is He, Lord, that I may believe in Him?"

[37]And Jesus said to him, "You have both seen Him and it is He who is talking with you."

[38]Then he said, "Lord, I believe!" And he worshiped Him.

[39]And Jesus said, "For judgment I have come into this world, that those who do not see may see, and that those who see may be made blind."

[40]Then *some* of the Pharisees who were with Him heard these words, and said to Him, "Are we blind also?"

[41]Jesus said to them, "If you were blind, you would have no sin; but now you say, 'We see.' Therefore your sin remains.

giving God glory

Jesus' disciples asked Him about a blind man—whether it was his or his parents' sin that caused him to be blind. This seems to be a familiar question, since we're always asking God why this or why that. His answer revealed a perspective on all of life that I wish I could hold onto

continued on next page

tighter. If Jesus said that everything happens so that the works of God may be revealed, does that still apply today? I have to believe it does—especially after watching some close friends go through the death of their baby. They knew all through the pregnancy that the baby was going to have some problems, but they still decided to carry it to term. When the baby was stillborn, I have to admit that it was very hard for me not to be angry with God. But this couple had the best attitude. They continually shared God's love with their friends and family. People are watching how we are going to react in hard times. Our witness gets validated as we experience God's love through our adversity.

Bob Herdman

How I'm seeing God's love through my adversities:

_____

_____

_____

_____

_____

_____

_____

_____

_____

_____

_____

_____

_____

"Neither this man nor his parents sinned, but that the works of God should be revealed in him."
(John 9:3)

JESUS COMES TO ZACCHAEUS' HOUSE

¹Then *Jesus* entered and passed through Jericho. ²Now behold, *there was* a man named Zacchaeus who was a chief tax collector, and he was rich. ³And he sought to see who Jesus was, but could not because of the crowd, for he was of short stature. ⁴So he ran ahead and climbed up into a sycamore tree to see Him, for He was going to pass that *way.* ⁵And when Jesus came to the place, He looked up and saw him, and said to him, "Zacchaeus, make haste and come down, for today I must stay at your house." ⁶So he made haste and came down, and received Him joyfully. ⁷But when they saw *it,* they all complained, saying, "He has gone to be a guest with a man who is a sinner."

⁸Then Zacchaeus stood and said to the Lord, "Look, Lord, I give half of my goods to the poor; and if I have taken anything from anyone by false accusation, I restore fourfold."

⁹And Jesus said to him, "Today salvation has come to this house, because he also is a son of Abraham; ¹⁰for the Son of Man has come to seek and to save that which was lost."

THE PARABLE OF THE MINAS

¹¹Now as they heard these things, He spoke another parable, because He was near Jerusalem and because they thought the kingdom of God would appear immediately. ¹²Therefore He said: "A certain nobleman went into a far country to receive for himself a kingdom and to return. ¹³So he called ten of his servants, delivered to them ten minas, and said to them, 'Do business till I come.' ¹⁴But his citizens hated him, and sent a delegation after him, saying, 'We will not have this *man* to reign over us.'

¹⁵"And so it was that when he returned, having received the kingdom, he then commanded these servants, to whom he had given the money, to be called to him, that he might know how much every man had gained by trading. ¹⁶Then came the first, saying, 'Master, your mina has earned ten minas.' ¹⁷And he said to him, 'Well *done,* good servant; because you were faithful in a very little, have authority over ten cities.' ¹⁸And the second came, saying, 'Master, your mina has earned five minas.' ¹⁹Likewise he said to him, 'You also be over five cities.'

²⁰"Then another came, saying, 'Master, here is your mina, which I have kept put away in a handkerchief. ²¹For I feared you, because you are an austere man. You collect what you did not deposit, and reap what you did not sow.' ²²And he said to him, 'Out of your own mouth I will judge you, *you* wicked servant. You knew that I was an austere man, collecting what I did not deposit and reaping what I did not sow. ²³Why then did you not put my money in the bank, that at my coming I might have collected it with interest?'

²⁴"And he said to those who stood by, 'Take the mina from him, and give *it* to him who has ten minas.' ²⁵(But they said to him, 'Master, he has ten minas.') ²⁶For I say to you, that to everyone who has will be given; and from him who does not have, even what he has will be taken

away from him. ²⁷But bring here those enemies of mine, who did not want me to reign over them, and slay *them* before me.' "

THE TRIUMPHAL ENTRY

²⁸When He had said this, He went on ahead, going up to Jerusalem. ²⁹And it came to pass, when He drew near to Bethphage and Bethany, at the mountain called Olivet, *that* He sent two of His disciples, ³⁰saying, "Go into the village opposite *you*, where as you enter you will find a colt tied, on which no one has ever sat. Loose it and bring *it here.* ³¹And if anyone asks you, 'Why are you loosing *it?*' thus you shall say to him, 'Because the Lord has need of it.' "

³²So those who were sent went their way and found *it* just as He had said to them. ³³But as they were loosing the colt, the owners of it said to them, "Why are you loosing the colt?"

³⁴And they said, "The Lord has need of him." ³⁵Then they brought him to Jesus. And they threw their own clothes on the colt, and they set Jesus on him. ³⁶And as He went, *many* spread their clothes on the road.

³⁷Then, as He was now drawing near the descent of the Mount of Olives, the whole multitude of the disciples began to rejoice and praise God with a loud voice for all the mighty works they had seen, ³⁸saying:

" 'Blessed *is* the King who comes in the name of the LORD!'
Peace in heaven and glory in the highest!"

³⁹And some of the Pharisees called to Him from the crowd, "Teacher, rebuke Your disciples."

⁴⁰But He answered and said to them, "I tell you that if these should keep silent, the stones would immediately cry out."

JESUS WEEPS OVER JERUSALEM

⁴¹Now as He drew near, He saw the city and wept over it, ⁴²saying, "If you had known, even you, especially in this your day, the things *that make* for your peace! But now they are hidden from your eyes. ⁴³For days will come upon you when your enemies will build an embankment around you, surround you and close you in on every side, ⁴⁴and level you, and your children within you, to the ground; and they will not leave in you one stone upon another, because you did not know the time of your visitation."

JESUS CLEANSES THE TEMPLE

⁴⁵Then He went into the temple and began to drive out those who bought and sold in it, ⁴⁶saying to them, "It is written, 'My house is a house of prayer,' but you have made it a 'den of thieves.' "

⁴⁷And He was teaching daily in the temple. But the chief priests, the scribes, and the leaders of the people sought to destroy Him, ⁴⁸and were unable to do anything; for all the people were very attentive to hear Him.

using our talents

The Bible guarantees that God has given each of us many gifts and talents. It's up to us to decide what we're going to do with them. God's desire is that we use them to build His kingdom, but instead many of us choose to sit quietly on the couch while we wait for His return. What has God given to you that you could use to further His kingdom here on earth? Whether you have talents as a musician, or as a doctor, a teacher, or whatever, God asks that your talents and gifts be used for His purposes. Popular evangelist Billy Graham is a great communicator. Many years ago he made the decision to use that gift for God's purposes and has gone on to impact the world in huge, seemingly impossible ways. Instead of falling into the trap of desiring the talent another person might possess, try to identify the way that God has uniquely gifted you to be used. How can God invade your day-to-day life, using your efforts and activities for His purposes?

Bob Herdman

How God is asking me to use my talents today:

_____

_____

_____

_____

_____

_____

_____

_____

"Well done, good servant; because you were faithful in a very little, have authority over ten cities." (Luke 19:17b)

JESUS' AUTHORITY QUESTIONED

¹Now it happened on one of those days, as He taught the people in the temple and preached the gospel, *that* the chief priests and the scribes, together with the elders, confronted Him ²and spoke to Him, saying, "Tell us, by what authority are You doing these things? Or who is he who gave You this authority?"

³But He answered and said to them, "I also will ask you one thing, and answer Me: ⁴The baptism of John—was it from heaven or from men?"

⁵And they reasoned among themselves, saying, "If we say, 'From heaven,' He will say, 'Why then did you not believe him?' ⁶But if we say, 'From men,' all the people will stone us, for they are persuaded that John was a prophet." ⁷So they answered that they did not know where *it was* from.

⁸And Jesus said to them, "Neither will I tell you by what authority I do these things."

THE PARABLE OF THE WICKED VINEDRESSERS

⁹Then He began to tell the people this parable: "A certain man planted a vineyard, leased it to vinedressers, and went into a far country for a long time. ¹⁰Now at vintage-time he sent a servant to the vinedressers, that they might give him some of the fruit of the vineyard. But the vinedressers beat him and sent *him* away empty-handed. ¹¹Again he sent another servant; and they beat him also, treated *him* shamefully, and sent *him* away empty-handed. ¹²And again he sent a third; and they wounded him also and cast *him* out.

¹³"Then the owner of the vineyard said, 'What shall I do? I will send my beloved son. Probably they will respect *him* when they see him.' ¹⁴But when the vinedressers saw him, they reasoned among themselves, saying, 'This is the heir. Come, let us kill him, that the inheritance may be ours.' ¹⁵So they cast him out of the vineyard and killed *him*. Therefore what will the owner of the vineyard do to them? ¹⁶He will come and destroy those vinedressers and give the vineyard to others."

And when they heard *it* they said, "Certainly not!"

¹⁷Then He looked at them and said, "What then is this that is written:

'The stone which the builders rejected
Has become the chief cornerstone'?

¹⁸Whoever falls on that stone will be broken; but on whomever it falls, it will grind him to powder."

¹⁹And the chief priests and the scribes that very hour sought to lay hands on Him, but they feared the people—for they knew He had spoken this parable against them.

THE PHARISEES: IS IT LAWFUL TO PAY TAXES TO CAESAR?

²⁰So they watched *Him*, and sent spies who pretended to be righteous, that they might seize on His words, in order to deliver Him to the power and the authority of the governor. ²¹Then they asked Him, saying, "Teacher, we know that You say and

teach rightly, and You do not show personal favoritism, but teach the way of God in truth: ²²Is it lawful for us to pay taxes to Caesar or not?"

²³But He perceived their craftiness, and said to them, "Why do you test Me? ²⁴Show Me a denarius. Whose image and inscription does it have?"

They answered and said, "Caesar's."

²⁵And He said to them, "Render therefore to Caesar the things that are Caesar's, and to God the things that are God's."

²⁶But they could not catch Him in His words in the presence of the people. And they marveled at His answer and kept silent.

THE SADDUCEES: WHAT ABOUT THE RESURRECTION?

²⁷Then some of the Sadducees, who deny that there is a resurrection, came to *Him* and asked Him, ²⁸saying: "Teacher, Moses wrote to us *that* if a man's brother dies, having a wife, and he dies without children, his brother should take his wife and raise up off–spring for his brother. ²⁹Now there were seven brothers. And the first took a wife, and died without chil–dren. ³⁰And the second took her as wife, and he died childless. ³¹Then the third took her, and in like manner the seven also; and they left no children, and died. ³²Last of all the woman died also. ³³Therefore, in the resurrection, whose wife does she become? For all seven had her as wife."

³⁴Jesus answered and said to them, "The sons of this age marry and are given in marriage. ³⁵But those who are counted worthy to attain that age, and the resurrection from the dead, neither marry nor are given in mar–riage; ³⁶nor can they die anymore, for they are equal to the angels and are sons of God, being sons of the resur–rection. ³⁷But even Moses showed in the *burning* bush *passage* that the dead are raised, when he called the Lord 'the God of Abraham, the God of Isaac, and the God of Jacob.' ³⁸For He is not the God of the dead but of the living, for all live to Him."

³⁹Then some of the scribes an–swered and said, "Teacher, You have spoken well." ⁴⁰But after that they dared not question Him anymore.

JESUS: HOW CAN DAVID CALL HIS DESCENDANT LORD?

⁴¹And He said to them, "How can they say that the Christ is the Son of David? ⁴²Now David himself said in the Book of Psalms:

'The LORD said to my Lord,
"Sit at My right hand,
⁴³ Till I make Your enemies Your
    footstool." '

⁴⁴Therefore David calls Him 'Lord'; how is He then his Son?"

BEWARE OF THE SCRIBES

⁴⁵Then, in the hearing of all the people, He said to His disciples, ⁴⁶"Be–ware of the scribes, who desire to go around in long robes, love greetings in the marketplaces, the best seats in the synagogues, and the best places at feasts, ⁴⁷who devour widows' houses, and for a pretense make long prayers. These will receive greater condemna–tion."

obey authority, honor God

Jesus was pretty clear about telling people to give to Caesar what is Caesar's and to God what is God's. Sometimes I think we get caught up into thinking that our government is responsible for the spiritual downfall of our country—that if we would just put money into legislating morality, then we would be able to change the heart of the country. If we just give to the government what they ask us to and then get busy concentrating our efforts on giving God's love and compassion to other people, that's when we'll start changing the world. In spite of the government's decision to eliminate prayer in schools, nobody can ever stop you from praying right where you are. We might think things are getting worse and worse, but nobody can ever take away the faith that we have. Nobody can ever tell you what you can or cannot believe—much less put any restrictions on the intimate relationship you have with the Savior. Our country is not going to make or break us as Christians. It comes down to our own personal relationship with Christ.

Bob Herdman

How I'm building my relationship with Christ today:

_____

_____

_____

_____

_____

_____

JESUS THE TRUE SHEPHERD

1"Most assuredly, I say to you, he who does not enter the sheepfold by the door, but climbs up some other way, the same is a thief and a robber. 2But he who enters by the door is the shepherd of the sheep. 3To him the doorkeeper opens, and the sheep hear his voice; and he calls his own sheep by name and leads them out. 4And when he brings out his own sheep, he goes before them; and the sheep follow him, for they know his voice. 5Yet they will by no means follow a stranger, but will flee from him, for they do not know the voice of strangers." 6Jesus used this illustration, but they did not understand the things which He spoke to them.

JESUS THE GOOD SHEPHERD

7Then Jesus said to them again, "Most assuredly, I say to you, I am the door of the sheep. 8All who *ever* came before Me are thieves and robbers, but the sheep did not hear them. 9I am the door. If anyone enters by Me, he will be saved, and will go in and out and find pasture. 10The thief does not come except to steal, and to kill, and to destroy. I have come that they may have life, and that they may have *it* more abundantly.

11"I am the good shepherd. The good shepherd gives His life for the sheep. 12But a hireling, *he who is* not the shepherd, one who does not own the sheep, sees the wolf coming and leaves the sheep and flees; and the wolf catches the sheep and scatters them. 13The hireling flees because he is a hireling and does not care about

the sheep. 14I am the good shepherd; and I know My *sheep*, and am known by My own. 15As the Father knows Me, even so I know the Father; and I lay down My life for the sheep. 16And other sheep I have which are not of this fold; them also I must bring, and they will hear My voice; and there will be one flock *and* one shepherd.

17"Therefore My Father loves Me, because I lay down My life that I may take it again. 18No one takes it from Me, but I lay it down of Myself. I have power to lay it down, and I have power to take it again. This command I have received from My Father."

19Therefore there was a division again among the Jews because of these sayings. 20And many of them said, "He has a demon and is mad. Why do you listen to Him?"

21Others said, "These are not the words of one who has a demon. Can a demon open the eyes of the blind?"

THE SHEPHERD KNOWS HIS SHEEP

22Now it was the Feast of Dedication in Jerusalem, and it was winter. 23And Jesus walked in the temple, in Solomon's porch. 24Then the Jews surrounded Him and said to Him, "How long do You keep us in doubt? If You are the Christ, tell us plainly."

25Jesus answered them, "I told you, and you do not believe. The works that I do in My Father's name, they bear witness of Me. 26But you do not believe, because you are not of My sheep, as I said to you. 27My sheep hear My voice, and I know them, and they follow Me. 28And I give them eternal life, and they shall never perish; neither shall anyone snatch them out of My hand. ²⁹My Father, who has given *them* to Me, is greater than all; and no one is able to snatch *them* out of My Father's hand. ³⁰I and *My* Father are one."

RENEWED EFFORTS TO STONE JESUS

³¹Then the Jews took up stones again to stone Him. ³²Jesus answered them, "Many good works I have shown you from My Father. For which of those works do you stone Me?"

³³The Jews answered Him, saying, "For a good work we do not stone You, but for blasphemy, and because You, being a Man, make Yourself God."

³⁴Jesus answered them, "Is it not written in your law, 'I said, "You are gods" '? ³⁵If He called them gods, to whom the word of God came (and the Scripture cannot be broken), ³⁶do you say of Him whom the Father sanctified and sent into the world, 'You are blaspheming,' because I said, 'I am the Son of God'? ³⁷If I do not do the works of My Father, do not believe Me; ³⁸but if I do, though you do not believe Me, believe the works, that you may know and believe that the Father *is* in Me, and I in Him." ³⁹Therefore they sought again to seize Him, but He escaped out of their hand.

THE BELIEVERS BEYOND JORDAN

⁴⁰And He went away again beyond the Jordan to the place where John was baptizing at first, and there He stayed. ⁴¹Then many came to Him and said, "John performed no sign, but all the things that John spoke about this Man were true." ⁴²And many believed in Him there.

accepting responsibility

DAY 25

John 10:12–13 talks about the hired hand that doesn't care about the wolf attacking the sheep because he doesn't own them. This seems to relate to how it's so easy to let things slide if they don't directly affect us, even when we see a need. You might have a friend who is doing something that you disagree with, or see a way they might be stumbling or falling, but you don't want to say anything for fear of losing the friendship. Sometimes I don't even take responsibility for my own life. You'd think I'd want what's best for my life, certain that God's way is best for me. But I still do things that are away from His desire for me. God will do

continued on next page

whatever He can to care for us, protecting and delivering us from anything that might attack us, if we seek Him for that help. Why is it so easy to think I can go my own way and not get eaten by the wolves? God, help me to accept more responsibility for my own life and also to know when I need to step in and help someone I care about.

Ben Herdman

How I'm taking up the challenge today:

"I am the good shepherd; and I know My sheep, and am known by My own."
(John 10:14)

THE DEATH OF LAZARUS

¹Now a certain *man* was sick, Lazarus of Bethany, the town of Mary and her sister Martha. ²It was *that* Mary who anointed the Lord with fragrant oil and wiped His feet with her hair, whose brother Lazarus was sick. ³Therefore the sisters sent to Him, saying, "Lord, behold, he whom You love is sick."

⁴When Jesus heard *that*, He said, "This sickness is not unto death, but for the glory of God, that the Son of God may be glorified through it."

⁵Now Jesus loved Martha and her sister and Lazarus. ⁶So, when He heard that he was sick, He stayed two more days in the place where He was. ⁷Then after this He said to *the* disciples, "Let us go to Judea again."

⁸*The* disciples said to Him, "Rabbi, lately the Jews sought to stone You, and are You going there again?"

⁹Jesus answered, "Are there not twelve hours in the day? If anyone walks in the day, he does not stumble, because he sees the light of this world. ¹⁰But if one walks in the night, he stumbles, because the light is not in him." ¹¹These things He said, and after that He said to them, "Our friend Lazarus sleeps, but I go that I may wake him up."

¹²Then His disciples said, "Lord, if he sleeps he will get well." ¹³However, Jesus spoke of his death, but they thought that He was speaking about taking rest in sleep.

¹⁴Then Jesus said to them plainly, "Lazarus is dead. ¹⁵And I am glad for your sakes that I was not there, that you may believe. Nevertheless let us go to him."

¹⁶Then Thomas, who is called the Twin, said to his fellow disciples, "Let us also go, that we may die with Him."

I AM THE RESURRECTION AND THE LIFE

¹⁷So when Jesus came, He found that he had already been in the tomb four days. ¹⁸Now Bethany was near Jerusalem, about two miles away. ¹⁹And many of the Jews had joined the women around Martha and Mary, to comfort them concerning their brother.

²⁰Now Martha, as soon as she heard that Jesus was coming, went and met Him, but Mary was sitting in the house. ²¹Now Martha said to Jesus, "Lord, if You had been here, my brother would not have died. ²²But even now I know that whatever You ask of God, God will give You."

²³Jesus said to her, "Your brother will rise again."

²⁴Martha said to Him, "I know that he will rise again in the resurrection at the last day."

²⁵Jesus said to her, "I am the resurrection and the life. He who believes in Me, though he may die, he shall live. ²⁶And whoever lives and believes in Me shall never die. Do you believe this?"

²⁷She said to Him, "Yes, Lord, I believe that You are the Christ, the Son of God, who is to come into the world."

JESUS AND DEATH, THE LAST ENEMY

²⁸And when she had said these things, she went her way and secretly

called Mary her sister, saying, "The Teacher has come and is calling for you." [29]As soon as she heard *that,* she arose quickly and came to Him. [30]Now Jesus had not yet come into the town, but was in the place where Martha met Him. [31]Then the Jews who were with her in the house, and comforting her, when they saw that Mary rose up quickly and went out, followed her, saying, "She is going to the tomb to weep there."

[32]Then, when Mary came where Jesus was, and saw Him, she fell down at His feet, saying to Him, "Lord, if You had been here, my brother would not have died."

[33]Therefore, when Jesus saw her weeping, and the Jews who came with her weeping, He groaned in the spirit and was troubled. [34]And He said, "Where have you laid him?"

They said to Him, "Lord, come and see."

[35]Jesus wept. [36]Then the Jews said, "See how He loved him!"

[37]And some of them said, "Could not this Man, who opened the eyes of the blind, also have kept this man from dying?"

LAZARUS RAISED FROM THE DEAD

[38]Then Jesus, again groaning in Himself, came to the tomb. It was a cave, and a stone lay against it. [39]Jesus said, "Take away the stone."

Martha, the sister of him who was dead, said to Him, "Lord, by this time there is a stench, for he has been *dead* four days."

[40]Jesus said to her, "Did I not say to you that if you would believe you would see the glory of God?" [41]Then they took away the stone *from the place* where the dead man was lying. And Jesus lifted up *His* eyes and said, "Father, I thank You that You have heard Me. [42]And I know that You always hear Me, but because of the people who are standing by I said *this,* that they may believe that You sent Me." [43]Now when He had said these things, He cried with a loud voice, "Lazarus, come forth!" [44]And he who had died came out bound hand and foot with graveclothes, and his face was wrapped with a cloth. Jesus said to them, "Loose him, and let him go."

THE PLOT TO KILL JESUS

[45]Then many of the Jews who had come to Mary, and had seen the things Jesus did, believed in Him. [46]But some of them went away to the Pharisees and told them the things Jesus did. [47]Then the chief priests and the Pharisees gathered a council and said, "What shall we do? For this Man works many signs. [48]If we let Him alone like this, everyone will believe in Him, and the Romans will come and take away both our place and nation."

[49]And one of them, Caiaphas, being high priest that year, said to them, "You know nothing at all, [50]nor do you consider that it is expedient for us that one man should die for the people, and not that the whole nation should perish." [51]Now this he did not say on his own *authority;* but being high priest that year he prophesied that Jesus would die for the nation, [52]and not for that nation only, but also that He would gather together in one the children of God who were scattered abroad.

[53]Then, from that day on, they plotted to put Him to death. [54]Therefore Jesus no longer walked openly among the Jews, but went from there into the country near the wilderness,

to a city called Ephraim, and there re-mained with His disciples.

⁵⁵And the Passover of the Jews was near, and many went from the country up to Jerusalem before the Passover, to purify themselves. ⁵⁶Then they sought Jesus, and spoke among themselves as they stood in the temple, "What do you think—that He will not come to the feast?" ⁵⁷Now both the chief priests and the Pharisees had given a command, that if anyone knew where He was, he should report *it*, that they might seize Him.

shouing compassion

J **ohn 11:35 says, "Jesus wept."** This just blows my mind. The short-est verse in the Bible is also one of the most revealing about the char-acter of Jesus. He already knew that Lazarus had died, and surely He knew that He was about to raise him from the dead. Yet He still wept when He saw the sadness of Lazarus's sisters and friends. He wanted to relate to them, to feel what they were feeling, so that His miracle would hold even greater significance and bring more glory to God. I want to have this kind of compassion that literally feels what another person is feeling, rather than thinking I could never do anything for a person who may be hurting. Instead of just judging someone, I want to pray for deeper understanding of his or her situation. I want to pray for broken-ness to be able to feel what they're feeling. Is there somebody you know right now that you can't understand what they're going through? Pray for Christ's compassion to invade your heart, and then be willing to reach out to them.

Will McGinniss

How Jesus is building compassion for others in my heart today:

_____

_____

_____

_____

_____

_____

_____

_____

_____

_____

_____

_____

_____

_____

_____

_____

_____

_____

_____

_____

_____

Jesus wept. Then the Jews
said, "See how He loved him!"
(John 11:35, 36)

JESUS PREDICTS THE DESTRUCTION OF THE TEMPLE

¹Then as He went out of the temple, one of His disciples said to Him, "Teacher, see what manner of stones and what buildings *are here!*"

²And Jesus answered and said to him, "Do you see these great buildings? Not *one* stone shall be left upon another, that shall not be thrown down."

THE SIGNS OF THE TIMES AND THE END OF THE AGE

³Now as He sat on the Mount of Olives opposite the temple, Peter, James, John, and Andrew asked Him privately, ⁴"Tell us, when will these things be? And what *will be* the sign when all these things will be fulfilled?"

⁵And Jesus, answering them, began to say: "Take heed that no one deceives you. ⁶For many will come in My name, saying, 'I am *He*,' and will deceive many. ⁷But when you hear of wars and rumors of wars, do not be troubled; for *such things* must happen, but the end *is* not yet. ⁸For nation will rise against nation, and kingdom against kingdom. And there will be earthquakes in various places, and there will be famines and troubles. These *are* the beginnings of sorrows.

⁹"But watch out for yourselves, for they will deliver you up to councils, and you will be beaten in the synagogues. You will be brought before rulers and kings for My sake, for a testimony to them. ¹⁰And the gospel must first be preached to all the nations. ¹¹But when they arrest *you* and deliver you up, do not worry beforehand, or premeditate what you will speak. But whatever is given you in that hour, speak that; for it is not you who speak, but the Holy Spirit. ¹²Now brother will betray brother to death, and a father *his* child; and children will rise up against parents and cause them to be put to death. ¹³And you will be hated by all for My name's sake. But he who endures to the end shall be saved.

THE GREAT TRIBULATION

¹⁴"So when you see the 'abomination of desolation,' spoken of by Daniel the prophet, standing where it ought not" (let the reader understand), "then let those who are in Judea flee to the mountains. ¹⁵Let him who is on the housetop not go down into the house, nor enter to take anything out of his house. ¹⁶And let him who is in the field not go back to get his clothes. ¹⁷But woe to those who are pregnant and to those who are nursing babies in those days! ¹⁸And pray that your flight may not be in winter. ¹⁹For *in* those days there will be tribulation, such as has not been since the beginning of the creation which God created until this time, nor ever shall be. ²⁰And unless the Lord had shortened those days, no flesh would be saved; but for the elect's sake, whom He chose, He shortened the days.

²¹"Then if anyone says to you, 'Look, here *is* the Christ!' or, 'Look, *He is* there!' do not believe it. ²²For false christs and false prophets will rise and show signs and wonders to de-

ceive, if possible, even the elect. ²³But take heed; see, I have told you all things beforehand.

THE COMING OF THE SON OF MAN

²⁴"But in those days, after that tribu-lation, the sun will be darkened, and the moon will not give its light; ²⁵the stars of heaven will fall, and the pow-ers in the heavens will be shaken. ²⁶Then they will see the Son of Man coming in the clouds with great power and glory. ²⁷And then He will send His angels, and gather together His elect from the four winds, from the farthest part of earth to the far-thest part of heaven.

THE PARABLE OF THE FIG TREE

²⁸"Now learn this parable from the fig tree: When its branch has already become tender, and puts forth leaves, you know that summer is near. ²⁹So you also, when you see these things happening, know that it is near—at the doors! ³⁰Assuredly, I say to you, this generation will by no means pass away till all these things take place. ³¹Heaven and earth will pass away, but My words will by no means pass away.

NO ONE KNOWS THE DAY OR HOUR

³²"But of that day and hour no one knows, not even the angels in heaven, nor the Son, but only the Father. ³³Take heed, watch and pray; for you do not know when the time is. ³⁴*It is* like a man going to a far country, who left his house and gave authority to his servants, and to each his work, and commanded the doorkeeper to watch. ³⁵Watch therefore, for you do not know when the master of the house is coming—in the evening, at midnight, at the crowing of the rooster, or in the morning— ³⁶lest, coming suddenly, he find you sleep-ing. ³⁷And what I say to you, I say to all: Watch!"

Jesus is coming!

I t was frightening to me growing up hearing people talk about God coming back. Those people seemed to know, in some magical way, what the day or time was going to be. Of course, they usually had some books or products that they were selling to go along with their prognosti-cations! Mark 13:32 has always been a comfort to me because it says that no one knows the day or the hour. If someone says that they do know, they're basically a false prophet, or a liar, really. It's so much better trust-

continued on next page

ing that only God knows the exact details of His return. The Bible says that Jesus doesn't even know! God is on His throne and is completely in control of the world's events. Even with all the scary things we go through in this life, people seem to be continually looking for an "escape hatch." They want something that will get them out of any trial. God promises that we will never be forced to endure more than we can handle, and that He will take us away when His time is right.

Mark Stuart

What God is showing me in His Word today:

_____

_____

_____

_____

_____

_____

_____

_____

_____

_____

_____

_____

_____

_____

"But of that day and hour no one knows, not even the angels in heaven, nor the Son, but only the Father."
(Mark 13:32)

THE PLOT TO KILL JESUS

¹Now the Feast of Unleavened Bread drew near, which is called Passover. ²And the chief priests and the scribes sought how they might kill Him, for they feared the people. ³Then Satan entered Judas, surnamed Iscariot, who was numbered among the twelve. ⁴So he went his way and conferred with the chief priests and captains, how he might betray Him to them. ⁵And they were glad, and agreed to give him money. ⁶So he promised and sought opportunity to betray Him to them in the absence of the multitude.

JESUS AND HIS DISCIPLES PREPARE THE PASSOVER

⁷Then came the Day of Unleavened Bread, when the Passover must be killed. ⁸And He sent Peter and John, saying, "Go and prepare the Passover for us, that we may eat." ⁹So they said to Him, "Where do You want us to prepare?" ¹⁰And He said to them, "Behold, when you have entered the city, a man will meet you carrying a pitcher of water; follow him into the house which he enters. ¹¹Then you shall say to the master of the house, 'The Teacher says to you, "Where is the guest room where I may eat the Passover with My disciples?" ' ¹²Then he will show you a large, furnished upper room; there make ready." ¹³So they went and found it just as He had said to them, and they prepared the Passover.

JESUS INSTITUTES THE LORD'S SUPPER

¹⁴When the hour had come, He sat down, and the twelve apostles with Him. ¹⁵Then He said to them, "With *fervent* desire I have desired to eat this Passover with you before I suffer; ¹⁶for I say to you, I will no longer eat of it until it is fulfilled in the kingdom of God."

¹⁷Then He took the cup, and gave thanks, and said, "Take this and divide *it* among yourselves; ¹⁸for I say to you, I will not drink of the fruit of the vine until the kingdom of God comes."

¹⁹And He took bread, gave thanks and broke *it*, and gave *it* to them, saying, "This is My body which is given for you; do this in remembrance of Me."

²⁰Likewise He also *took* the cup after supper, saying, "This cup *is* the new covenant in My blood, which is shed for you. ²¹But behold, the hand of My betrayer *is* with Me on the table. ²²And truly the Son of Man goes as it has been determined, but woe to that man by whom He is betrayed!"

²³Then they began to question among themselves, which of them it was who would do this thing.

THE DISCIPLES ARGUE ABOUT GREATNESS

²⁴Now there was also a dispute among them, as to which of them should be considered the greatest. ²⁵And He said to them, "The kings of the Gentiles exercise lordship over them, and those who exercise author-

ity over them are called 'benefactors.' [26]But not so *among* you; on the contrary, he who is greatest among you, let him be as the younger, and he who governs as he who serves. [27]For who *is* greater, he who sits at the table, or he who serves? *Is* it not he who sits at the table? Yet I am among you as the One who serves.

[28]"But you are those who have continued with Me in My trials. [29]And I bestow upon you a kingdom, just as My Father bestowed *one* upon Me, [30]that you may eat and drink at My table in My kingdom, and sit on thrones judging the twelve tribes of Israel."

JESUS PREDICTS PETER'S DENIAL

[31]And the Lord said, "Simon, Simon! Indeed, Satan has asked for you, that he may sift *you* as wheat. [32]But I have prayed for you, that your faith should not fail; and when you have returned to *Me,* strengthen your brethren."

[33]But he said to Him, "Lord, I am ready to go with You, both to prison and to death."

[34]Then He said, "I tell you, Peter, the rooster shall not crow this day before you will deny three times that you know Me."

SUPPLIES FOR THE ROAD

[35]And He said to them, "When I sent you without money bag, knapsack, and sandals, did you lack anything?"

So they said, "Nothing."

[36]Then He said to them, "But now, he who has a money bag, let him take *it,* and likewise a knapsack; and he who has no sword, let him sell his garment and buy one. [37]For I say to you that this which is written must still be accomplished in Me: 'And He was numbered with the transgressors.' For the things concerning Me have an end."

[38]So they said, "Lord, look, here *are* two swords."

And He said to them, "It is enough."

THE PRAYER IN THE GARDEN

[39]Coming out, He went to the Mount of Olives, as He was accustomed, and His disciples also followed Him. [40]When He came to the place, He said to them, "Pray that you may not enter into temptation."

[41]And He was withdrawn from them about a stone's throw, and He knelt down and prayed, [42]saying, "Father, if it is Your will, take this cup away from Me; nevertheless not My will, but Yours, be done." [43]Then an angel appeared to Him from heaven, strengthening Him. [44]And being in agony, He prayed more earnestly. Then His sweat became like great drops of blood falling down to the ground.

[45]When He rose up from prayer, and had come to His disciples, He found them sleeping from sorrow. [46]Then He said to them, "Why do you sleep? Rise and pray, lest you enter into temptation."

BETRAYAL AND ARREST IN GETHSEMANE

[47]And while He was still speaking, behold, a multitude; and he who was called Judas, one of the twelve, went before them and drew near to Jesus to kiss Him. [48]But Jesus said to him, "Judas, are you betraying the Son of Man with a kiss?"

[49]When those around Him saw what was going to happen, they said to Him, "Lord, shall we strike with the sword?" [50]And one of them struck the

servant of the high priest and cut off his right ear.

⁵¹But Jesus answered and said, "Permit even this." And He touched his ear and healed him.

⁵²Then Jesus said to the chief priests, captains of the temple, and the elders who had come to Him, "Have you come out, as against a robber, with swords and clubs? ⁵³When I was with you daily in the temple, you did not try to seize Me. But this is your hour, and the power of darkness."

PETER DENIES JESUS, AND WEEPS BITTERLY

⁵⁴Having arrested Him, they led *Him* and brought Him into the high priest's house. But Peter followed at a distance. ⁵⁵Now when they had kindled a fire in the midst of the courtyard and sat down together, Peter sat among them. ⁵⁶And a certain servant girl, seeing him as he sat by the fire, looked intently at him and said, "This man was also with Him."

⁵⁷But he denied Him, saying, "Woman, I do not know Him."

⁵⁸And after a little while another saw him and said, "You also are of them."

But Peter said, "Man, I am not!"

⁵⁹Then after about an hour had passed, another confidently affirmed, saying, "Surely this *fellow* also was with Him, for he is a Galilean."

⁶⁰But Peter said, "Man, I do not know what you are saying!"

Immediately, while he was still speaking, the rooster crowed. ⁶¹And the Lord turned and looked at Peter. Then Peter remembered the word of the Lord, how He had said to him, "Before the rooster crows, you will deny Me three times." ⁶²So Peter went out and wept bitterly.

JESUS MOCKED AND BEATEN

⁶³Now the men who held Jesus mocked Him and beat Him. ⁶⁴And having blindfolded Him, they struck Him on the face and asked Him, saying, "Prophesy! Who is the one who struck You?" ⁶⁵And many other things they blasphemously spoke against Him.

JESUS FACES THE SANHEDRIN

⁶⁶As soon as it was day, the elders of the people, both chief priests and scribes, came together and led Him into their council, saying, ⁶⁷"If You are the Christ, tell us."

But He said to them, "If I tell you, you will by no means believe. ⁶⁸And if I also ask *you*, you will by no means answer Me or let *Me* go. ⁶⁹Hereafter the Son of Man will sit on the right hand of the power of God."

⁷⁰Then they all said, "Are You then the Son of God?"

So He said to them, "You *rightly* say that I am."

⁷¹And they said, "What further testimony do we need? For we have heard it ourselves from His own mouth."

thy will be done

I see an intense side of Jesus in the description of the agony He was going through knowing He was about to be killed. He was facing a challenge so monumental that He literally sweat drops of blood while He prayed. He was so human in this moment. In spite of the agony, He chose to accept God's will. As you make hard choices to follow God's will, find strength in Christ who suffered through the acceptance of His Father's will. I've been a Christian long enough that it can be easy to lose sight of the amazing greatness of what Jesus did for me. So often I say that I'm saved, but it doesn't make me weep when I think about what Christ went through to make that possible. As I consider all that Christ has done for me, I want to pray for more emotion, to have my heart pricked, and to not be so calloused and jaded. I want to have my faith be as new as it was when I first became a Christian and had all the baggage of sin lifted off of me.

Will McGinniss

What Jesus is showing me about Himself today:

_____

_____

_____

_____

_____

_____

_____

_____

And being in agony, He prayed more earnestly. Then His sweat became like great drops of blood falling down to the ground.
(Luke 22:44)

JESUS HANDED OVER TO PONTIUS PILATE

¹When morning came, all the chief priests and elders of the people plotted against Jesus to put Him to death. ²And when they had bound Him, they led Him away and delivered Him to Pontius Pilate the governor.

JUDAS HANGS HIMSELF

³Then Judas, His betrayer, seeing that He had been condemned, was remorseful and brought back the thirty pieces of silver to the chief priests and elders, ⁴saying, "I have sinned by betraying innocent blood."

And they said, "What *is that* to us? You see *to it!*"

⁵Then he threw down the pieces of silver in the temple and departed, and went and hanged himself.

⁶But the chief priests took the silver pieces and said, "It is not lawful to put them into the treasury, because they are the price of blood." ⁷And they consulted together and bought with them the potter's field, to bury strangers in. ⁸Therefore that field has been called the Field of Blood to this day.

⁹Then was fulfilled what was spoken by Jeremiah the prophet, saying, "And they took the thirty pieces of silver, the value of Him who was priced, whom they of the children of Israel priced, ¹⁰and gave them for the potter's field, as the LORD directed me."

JESUS FACES PILATE

¹¹Now Jesus stood before the governor. And the governor asked Him, saying, "Are You the King of the Jews?"

Jesus said to him, "*It is as* you say." ¹²And while He was being accused by the chief priests and elders, He answered nothing.

¹³Then Pilate said to Him, "Do You not hear how many things they testify against You?" ¹⁴But He answered him not one word, so that the governor marveled greatly.

TAKING THE PLACE OF BARABBAS

¹⁵Now at the feast the governor was accustomed to releasing to the multitude one prisoner whom they wished. ¹⁶And at that time they had a notorious prisoner called Barabbas. ¹⁷Therefore, when they had gathered together, Pilate said to them, "Whom do you want me to release to you? Barabbas, or Jesus who is called Christ?" ¹⁸For he knew that they had handed Him over because of envy.

¹⁹While he was sitting on the judgment seat, his wife sent to him, saying, "Have nothing to do with that just Man, for I have suffered many things today in a dream because of Him."

²⁰But the chief priests and elders persuaded the multitudes that they should ask for Barabbas and destroy Jesus. ²¹The governor answered and said to them, "Which of the two do you want me to release to you?"

They said, "Barabbas!"

²²Pilate said to them, "What then shall I do with Jesus who is called Christ?"

They all said to him, "Let Him be crucified!"

²³Then the governor said, "Why, what evil has He done?"

But they cried out all the more, saying, "Let Him be crucified!"

24When Pilate saw that he could not prevail at all, but rather *that* a tumult was rising, he took water and washed *his* hands before the multitude, saying, "I am innocent of the blood of this just Person. You see *to it.*"

25And all the people answered and said, "His blood *be* on us and on our children."

26Then he released Barabbas to them; and when he had scourged Jesus, he delivered *Him* to be crucified.

THE SOLDIERS MOCK JESUS

27Then the soldiers of the governor took Jesus into the Praetorium and gathered the whole garrison around Him. 28And they stripped Him and put a scarlet robe on Him. 29When they had twisted a crown of thorns, they put *it* on His head, and a reed in His right hand. And they bowed the knee before Him and mocked Him, saying, "Hail, King of the Jews!" 30Then they spat on Him, and took the reed and struck Him on the head. 31And when they had mocked Him, they took the robe off Him, put His *own* clothes on Him, and led Him away to be crucified.

THE KING ON A CROSS

32Now as they came out, they found a man of Cyrene, Simon by name. Him they compelled to bear His cross. 33And when they had come to a place called Golgotha, that is to say, Place of a Skull, 34they gave Him sour wine mingled with gall to drink. But when He had tasted *it*, He would not drink.

35Then they crucified Him, and divided His garments, casting lots, that it might be fulfilled which was spoken by the prophet:

"They divided My garments among them,
And for My clothing they cast lots."

36Sitting down, they kept watch over Him there. 37And they put up over His head the accusation written against Him:

THIS IS JESUS THE KING OF THE JEWS.

38Then two robbers were crucified with Him, one on the right and another on the left.

39And those who passed by blasphemed Him, wagging their heads 40and saying, "You who destroy the temple and build *it* in three days, save Yourself! If You are the Son of God, come down from the cross."

41Likewise the chief priests also mocking with the scribes and elders, said, 42"He saved others; Himself He cannot save. If He is the King of Israel, let Him now come down from the cross, and we will believe Him. 43He trusted in God; let Him deliver Him now if He will have Him; for He said, 'I am the Son of God.' "

44Even the robbers who were crucified with Him reviled Him with the same thing.

JESUS DIES ON THE CROSS

45Now from the sixth hour until the ninth hour there was darkness over all the land. 46And about the ninth hour Jesus cried out with a loud voice, saying, "Eli, Eli, lama sabachthani?" that is, "My God, My God, why have You forsaken Me?"

47Some of those who stood there, when they heard *that*, said, "This Man is calling for Elijah!" 48Immediately one of them ran and took a sponge filled *it* with sour wine and put *it* on a reed, and offered it to Him to drink. [49]The rest said, "Let Him alone; let us see if Elijah will come to save Him."

[50]And Jesus cried out again with a loud voice, and yielded up His spirit.

[51]Then, behold, the veil of the temple was torn in two from top to bottom; and the earth quaked, and the rocks were split, [52]and the graves were opened; and many bodies of the saints who had fallen asleep were raised; [53]and coming out of the graves after His resurrection, they went into the holy city and appeared to many.

[54]So when the centurion and those with him, who were guarding Jesus, saw the earthquake and the things that had happened, they feared greatly, saying, "Truly this was the Son of God!"

[55]And many women who followed Jesus from Galilee, ministering to Him, were there looking on from afar, [56]among whom were Mary Magdalene, Mary the mother of James and Joses, and the mother of Zebedee's sons.

JESUS BURIED IN JOSEPH'S TOMB

[57]Now when evening had come, there came a rich man from Arimathea, named Joseph, who himself had also become a disciple of Jesus. [58]This man went to Pilate and asked for the body of Jesus. Then Pilate commanded the body to be given to him. [59]When Joseph had taken the body, he wrapped it in a clean linen cloth, [60]and laid it in his new tomb which he had hewn out of the rock; and he rolled a large stone against the door of the tomb, and departed. [61]And Mary Magdalene was there, and the other Mary, sitting opposite the tomb.

PILATE SETS A GUARD

[62]On the next day, which followed the Day of Preparation, the chief priests and Pharisees gathered together to Pilate, [63]saying, "Sir, we remember, while He was still alive, how that deceiver said, 'After three days I will rise.' [64]Therefore command that the tomb be made secure until the third day, lest His disciples come by night and steal Him *away*, and say to the people, 'He has risen from the dead.' So the last deception will be worse than the first."

[65]Pilate said to them, "You have a guard; go your way, make *it* as secure as you know how." [66]So they went and made the tomb secure, sealing the stone and setting the guard.

the ultimate hope

DAY 29

The ultimate hope we have as Christians comes through a horribly grizzly execution. By dying on the Cross, Christ chose to accept the blame and punishment for the sin of all people throughout eternity. The fact that He died and then rose from the grave is proof that He wasn't just

continued on next page

man—He was indeed God. The acceptance of the truth of this passage is what we are first called to believe in order to be in relationship with the God of the Universe. Because of Christ's death and resurrection, God offers us an opportunity to live eternally. He's waiting to give His free gift to anyone who will believe. When we believe that Christ died on the Cross and came back to life on the third day, and accept His offer of forgiveness for our sin, we are then entitled to let Christ live His life through us. We crucify our own will and desires so that He has room to live in us. We hand over to Him our need to live our own life, and in return He gives us life that is so much greater than we could've ever dreamed.

Bob Herdman

How I'm letting Christ live through me today:

_____

_____

_____

_____

_____

_____

_____

_____

_____

_____

_____

_____

_____

"Truly this was the Son of God!"
(Matthew 27:54b)

HE IS RISEN

¹Now on the first *day* of the week, very early in the morning, they, and certain *other women* with them, came to the tomb bringing the spices which they had prepared. ²But they found the stone rolled away from the tomb. ³Then they went in and did not find the body of the Lord Jesus. ⁴And it happened, as they were greatly perplexed about this, that behold, two men stood by them in shining garments. ⁵Then, as they were afraid and bowed *their* faces to the earth, they said to them, "Why do you seek the living among the dead? ⁶He is not here, but is risen! Remember how He spoke to you when He was still in Galilee, ⁷saying, 'The Son of Man must be delivered into the hands of sinful men, and be crucified, and the third day rise again.' "

⁸And they remembered His words. ⁹Then they returned from the tomb and told all these things to the eleven and to all the rest. ¹⁰It was Mary Magdalene, Joanna, Mary *the mother* of James, and the other *women* with them, who told these things to the apostles. ¹¹And their words seemed to them like idle tales, and they did not believe them. ¹²But Peter arose and ran to the tomb; and stooping down, he saw the linen cloths lying by themselves; and he departed, marveling to himself at what had happened.

THE ROAD TO EMMAUS

¹³Now behold, two of them were traveling that same day to a village called Emmaus, which was seven miles from Jerusalem. ¹⁴And they talked together of all these things which had happened. ¹⁵So it was, while they conversed and reasoned, that Jesus Himself drew near and went with them. ¹⁶But their eyes were restrained, so that they did not know Him.

¹⁷And He said to them, "What kind of conversation *is* this that you have with one another as you walk and are sad?"

¹⁸Then the one whose name was Cleopas answered and said to Him, "Are You the only stranger in Jerusalem, and have You not known the things which happened there in these days?"

¹⁹And He said to them, "What things?"

So they said to Him, "The things concerning Jesus of Nazareth, who was a Prophet mighty in deed and word before God and all the people, ²⁰and how the chief priests and our rulers delivered Him to be condemned to death, and crucified Him. ²¹But we were hoping that it was He who was going to redeem Israel. Indeed, besides all this, today is the third day since these things happened. ²²Yes, and certain women of our company, who arrived at the tomb early, astonished us. ²³When they did not find His body, they came saying that they had also seen a vision of angels who said He was alive. ²⁴And certain of those *who were* with us went to the tomb and found *it* just as the women had said; but Him they did not see."

²⁵Then He said to them, "O foolish ones, and slow of heart to believe in all that the prophets have spoken!

²⁶Ought not the Christ to have suffered these things and to enter into His glory?" ²⁷And beginning at Moses and all the Prophets, He expounded to them in all the Scriptures the things concerning Himself.

THE DISCIPLES' EYES OPENED

²⁸Then they drew near to the village where they were going, and He indicated that He would have gone farther. ²⁹But they constrained Him, saying, "Abide with us, for it is toward evening, and the day is far spent." And He went in to stay with them. ³⁰Now it came to pass, as He sat at the table with them, that He took bread, blessed and broke *it*, and gave it to them. ³¹Then their eyes were opened and they knew Him; and He vanished from their sight.

³²And they said to one another, "Did not our heart burn within us while He talked with us on the road, and while He opened the Scriptures to us?" ³³So they rose up that very hour and returned to Jerusalem, and found the eleven and those *who were* with them gathered together, ³⁴saying, "The Lord is risen indeed, and has appeared to Simon!" ³⁵And they told about the things *that had happened* on the road, and how He was known to them in the breaking of bread.

JESUS APPEARS TO HIS DISCIPLES

³⁶Now as they said these things, Jesus Himself stood in the midst of them, and said to them, "Peace to you." ³⁷But they were terrified and frightened, and supposed they had seen a spirit.. ³⁸And He said to them, "Why are you troubled? And why do doubts arise in your hearts? ³⁹Behold My hands and My feet, that it is I Myself. Handle Me and see, for a spirit does not have flesh and bones as you see I have."

⁴⁰When He had said this, He showed them His hands and His feet. ⁴¹But while they still did not believe for joy, and marveled, He said to them, "Have you any food here?" ⁴²So they gave Him a piece of a broiled fish and some honeycomb. ⁴³And He took *it* and ate in their presence.

THE SCRIPTURES OPENED

⁴⁴Then He said to them, "These *are* the words which I spoke to you while I was still with you, that all things must be fulfilled which were written in the Law of Moses and *the* Prophets and *the* Psalms concerning Me." ⁴⁵And He opened their understanding, that they might comprehend the Scriptures.

⁴⁶Then He said to them, "Thus it is written, and thus it was necessary for the Christ to suffer and to rise from the dead the third day, ⁴⁷and that repentance and remission of sins should be preached in His name to all nations, beginning at Jerusalem. ⁴⁸And you are witnesses of these things. ⁴⁹Behold, I send the Promise of My Father upon you; but tarry in the city of Jerusalem until you are endued with power from on high."

THE ASCENSION

⁵⁰And He led them out as far as Bethany, and He lifted up His hands and blessed them. ⁵¹Now it came to pass, while He blessed them, that He was parted from them and carried up into heaven. ⁵²And they worshiped Him, and returned to Jerusalem with great joy, ⁵³and were continually in the temple praising and blessing God. Amen.

the most extreme love

Easter has always been an incredible time of the year for me. Of course, as kids it's easy to be distracted by the fact that there's always some kind of chocolate bunnies around. But it's more than that for me. Not only was I actually born on Easter Sunday, but that day also gives me such a powerful opportunity to come face to face with the reality of what Christ endured and overcame for my sake. It's amazing to think that even though Jesus continually told the disciples that He was going to come back from the dead, they didn't completely get it in their heads. Even today we have a hard time understanding how an actual man could be God at the same time. We downplay the fact that death has literally lost its sting. This is a very promising passage that can be a constant reminder to us that Jesus Christ has overcome death. Sure, I may have been born on Easter Sunday. But what we all celebrate on Easter Sunday—that Christ died and rose from the dead—means that we will never have to be defeated by death. That's worth celebrating!

Mark Stuart

How I'm celebrating Jesus' love for me today:

_____

_____

_____

_____

_____

_____